the book and the map

the Book and the map

New Insights into Book of Mormon Geography

VENICE PRIDDIS

ILLUSTRATIONS BY CHRISTOPHER PRIDDIS
MAPS BY ANNETTE PRIDDIS

Salt Lake City, Utah

COPYRIGHT © 1975 BY
BOOKCRAFT, INC.

COPYRIGHT © 1983 BY
VENICE PRIDDIS

All rights reserved

No part of this book may be reproduced in any manner whatsoever without written permission from the publisher, except in the case of brief quotations embodied in critical articles and reviews.

Library of Congress Catalog Card Number: 75-4326
ISBN 0-88494-277-5

8th Printing, 1983

Lithographed in the United States of America
PUBLISHERS PRESS
Salt Lake City, Utah

Contents

Maps vii
Publisher's Foreword ix
Preface xi
Acknowledgments xiii

    Introduction: Basic Geographical Relationships 1

PART I — ISLE OR CONTINENT
  1. Isle or Continent 9

PART II — THE LAND NORTHWARD
  2. The Narrow Neck 23
  3. Jaredite Lands 33
  4. Jaredite War Zones 49

PART III — THE LAND SOUTHWARD
  5. Lands Nephi-Lehi 63
  6. Escape from the Land Nephi 86
  7. Zarahemla 99

PART IV — FROM ISHMAEL TO CUMORAH
  8. Anti-Nephi-Lehi 115
  9. Nephite War Zones 125
 10. The Land Changed 141
 11. Mormon, Moroni and Cumorah 153

Bibliography 159
Index 163

Maps

Basic Geographical Relationships of Book of Mormon Lands	2
South America	11
Probable Geophysical Configuration of South America Before the Time of Christ	17
Two Non-Qualifying Isthmuses	25
The Narrow Neck of Land	28
Inter-Andean Highlands	36
Omer's Journey	42
Jaredite War Zones	51
Hill Ramah-Hill Cumorah	58
Coriantumr's Wanderings	59
Lehi's Landing — Nephi's Probable Trek	66
Inca Roads	69
Original Boundaries of the County Land of Nephi	74
The Original Land of Nephi and the Combined Lands of Nephi-Lehi	75
Mosiah's Escape to Zarahemla	79
Modern Names of Book of Mormon Lands	87
Escape into Wilderness by Amulon and Fellow Priests	89
Alma's Escape to Helam	92
The Search for the Land of Zarahemla	94
King Limhi's Escape Route	95
Alma's Escape to Zarahemla	97
Zarahemla and the Sidon River	102
The Battle of the Nephites and the Amlicites	105
Ammonihah Is Destroyed	110
King's Lands	122
Battle with the Zoramite-Led Lamanites	127
East Wilderness	128
Cities Taken by the Lamanites in the East Wilderness	131
Mulek Retaken by Stratagem	136
Bountiful	138
The Fighting by the West Sea	139
Migration of the People	143
The Great Wall	148

Publisher's Foreword

A good many books have been published on Book of Mormon geography, and a publisher should consider well before adding to their number.

First, the present book has the virtue of uniqueness as regards its geographical stand. Second, the location here indicated for that basic feature, the narrow neck of land, represents an imaginative piece of detection. Third, the author has done an unusual job of research in assembling her evidence and defining Book of Mormon lands and cities. Fourth, to those who accept the possibility of two Cumorahs (as many do) the basic conclusions of this book may seem at least plausible and logical. And fifth, the first four reasons argue that the author deserves a vehicle by which to bring her work to the attention of the interested reader. Bookcraft is pleased to provide that vehicle.

Both publisher and author are conscious of the many statements made by early Brethren which bear on Book of Mormon geography. It is doubtful that any geographical concept could fully reconcile all these statements, even where the precise wording is established; and in addition there is the matter of differing possibilities of interpretation, as well as the degree of inspiration, either human or divine, which prompted any particular statement. As to her own book, the present author was more than willing to offer a reconciliation of such statements in the context of her conclusions, but this would have made the book larger and costlier without necessarily improving its value.

The Book and the Map offers the reader some new and interesting insights into Book of Mormon geography. A book on this topic ought not to do less; and in the absence of a revelation on the subject, perhaps it cannot be faulted for not doing more.

Preface

Eight years of teaching seminary gave me an overwhelming desire to discover the lands and cities of the Book of Mormon. I read many books and articles on Book of Mormon geography. I used the seminary maps given me as teaching aids. None were satisfactory. I wanted to know the real geography of the Book of Mormon, not some proposed locations. Out of sheer desperation I decided to search for these places myself.

I was lucky — or blessed. After much prayer and study I stumbled onto the very clue that led to the discovery of those lands. It opened new understandings for me. I began to know the Jaredites and the Nephites as I had never known them before. It gave me some idea of the type of clothing they wore, the kind of food they ate. Best of all, I knew where they had traveled. It was fascinating, exciting.

After years of preparation, the manuscript for this book was in completed form and with the publisher when in October 1974 I made another discovery. It was then that, through Dr. Paul R. Cheesman's 1974 book *These Early Americans,* Verla Birrell's long-out-of-print *Book of Mormon Guide Book,* published in 1946, first came to my attention. It was then I learned that the idea of the location I indicate for the narrow neck of land, the most basic geographical feature, was not original with me as I had supposed, but that Verla Birrell had perceptively suggested that area as one of several possibilities. It would seem then that my major contribution has been to bring focus to that concept and, by independent research, support it and the pattern it brings to Book of Mormon geography by a body of evidence much of which was not available back in 1946.

Having made my geographical discoveries, I wanted others to share the thrill. This book is the outcome of that desire. It is my hope that it will induce in its readers the same excitement, the same insights into the Book of Mormon, that my quest has brought me.

Acknowledgments

I am indebted to many for the information contained in the printed sources and personal letters which have formed the basis of my research and which are listed in the footnotes and the bibliography. I view with particular admiration the numerous explorers and archaeologists who have waded through jungle and desert, traversed giant rivers, clambered up mountainsides, and braved dangerous insects, snakes, extremes of heat and cold and other rigors of the trail to uncover and record the wonders of the South American lands.

I am indebted also to my sons Bob and Ron Priddis for their many suggestions and persistent help; to my daughter-in-law Annette, for the maps in this book; to my son Christopher, for the illustrations; to my brother David Martin, for his consistent encouragement; and to Bookcraft editor George Bickerstaff for his direction and counsel and his editing of the manuscript.

Special thanks to my husband Alfred Priddis for the unfailing patience he exhibited over the years while I worked long hours on this book.

Most of all I am indebted to those ancient prophets who, under inspiration, wrote into what is primarily a religious record sufficient geographical information to make it possible to define the ancient lands on the modern map.

INTRODUCTION

Basic Geographical Relationships

Many readers will already be familiar with the basic geographical relationships of the places referred to in the Book of Mormon record. For those who are not, I have compiled the information contained in this Introduction and the accompanying map-chart. The source of this material is the Book of Mormon, either its direct statements or logical deductions from them. (The occasional unsupported conclusion will be apparent from its wording.) The chart merely shows directions, not proportions, since the latter are not ascertainable from the Book of Mormon.

Land Northward — Narrow Neck of Land — Land Southward

It is clearly stated in the Book of Mormon that there was a land northward and a land southward with a connecting link between called a narrow neck or small neck of land. (Alma 22:32; 63:5; Ether 10:20.) This land-bridge is a major key to Book of Mormon geography.

A careful reading of Alma 22:31-32 shows not only that "the land southward" was separated from "the land northward" by "a small neck of land," but that there the land of Desolation on the north met the land of Bountiful on the south. Thus the land of Bountiful was the northern part of the land southward. This is further borne out by the statement, ". . . the Nephites possessing all the land northward, yea, even all the land which was northward of the land Bountiful, according to their pleasure." (Alma 50:11.)

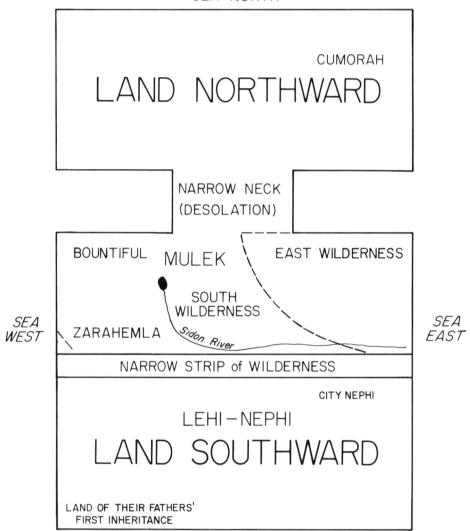

Lands Bountiful, Zarahemla, and Nephi

That Bountiful was on the west side of the land southward by the narrow neck of land is demonstrated by the following: "... Hagoth ... built him an exceedingly large ship, on the borders of the land Bountiful, by the land Desolation, and launched it forth into the west sea, by the narrow neck which led into the land northward." (Alma 63:5.)

Alma 22:27-29 establishes for us some further relative locations. Speaking in the context of the proclamation of the Lamanite king made in the land of Nephi, it places the land of Zarahemla "on the north" (i.e., north of the land of Nephi, which the Lamanites occupied). A narrow strip of wilderness running "from the sea east even to the sea west" divided the land of Nephi from the land of Zarahemla (verse 27). It further states that "the Nephites had taken possession of all the northern parts of the land bordering on the wilderness, at the head of the river Sidon, from the east to the west ... on the north, even until they came to the land which they called Bountiful" (verse 29).

Scriptures thus far quoted establish that the land of Bountiful, the land of Zarahemla and the land of Nephi were all part of the land southward, the land of Zarahemla being to the south of the land Bountiful and the land of Nephi being to the south of the land of Zarahemla.

Alma 22:28 records that Lamanites were living "on the west ... in the place of their fathers' first inheritance, and thus bordering along by the [western] seashore." "Their fathers" were Laman and Lemuel, who remained broadly in the area of Lehi's landing when the fleeing Nephi journeyed "in the wilderness for the space of many days." (2 Nephi 5:7.) "In the wilderness" suggests that Nephi's party fled inland, i.e., eastwards, away from the coastal strip in which pursuit would have been easy.

Inasmuch as, centuries later, the Nephites "came down" from the land of Nephi to the land of Zarahemla (Omni 12-13), their land apparently had been in the mountains. And since the land of Nephi was separated from the land of

Zarahemla by a narrow strip of wilderness, they were somewhere south of that strip. All this suggests the location of their land as the northeastern quarter of the land of Lehi-Nephi, the southern division of the land southward.

Lands Lehi and Mulek

Around 28 B.C. the greater part of the Lamanites had been converted to the gospel, and this brought about a complete freedom of movement between Nephite and Lamanite lands. In outlining this situation the record says: "Now the land south was called Lehi and the land north was called Mulek, . . . for the Lord did bring Mulek into the land north, and Lehi into the land south." (Helaman 6:10.)

The phraseology was no mistake. A few verses previously the chronicler had deliberately referred to "the land northward." (Helaman 6:6.) By "the land north" he meant the area north of the narrow strip of wilderness which divided the land of Nephi from the land of Zarahemla, the area to which the Lord had brought the Mulekites and where Mosiah discovered them. (See Omni 13, 16.) Thus the land southward (which as we have seen included the lands of Bountiful, Zarahemla and Nephi) had two general divisions — Mulek in the north and Lehi (sometimes referred to also as the land of Nephi or of Lehi-Nephi) in the south.

South Wilderness

Alma 31:3 refers to the land of Antionum as being east of the land of Zarahemla. Antionum "lay nearly bordering upon the seashore" and, according to the description in this verse, seems to have been close to the South Wilderness. Thus the South Wilderness is placed on our map-chart east of the land of Zarahemla and north of the narrow strip of wilderness which separated that land from the land of Lehi-Nephi.

East Wilderness

Alma 50:7-11 tells how Moroni's armies drove "the Lamanites who were in the east wilderness into their own lands, which were south of the land of Zarahemla," the East Wilderness being "north of the lands of their own possessions" (verse 9). The inhabitants of the land of Zarahemla then went "forth into the east wilderness, even to the borders by the [eastern] seashore" (verse 9) to possess the land. Then Moroni fortified the Nephites' southern border, "the line between the Nephites and the Lamanites, between the land of Zarahemla and the land of Nephi" (verse 11).

Clearly then the East Wilderness was north of the Zarahemla/Nephi border. Since there was also a South Wilderness (see above) which bordered upon a land east of the land of Zarahemla (Alma 31:3), the East Wilderness must have been more northerly than the South Wilderness, probably extending to an area east of the land Bountiful.

Sidon River

The Sidon river "ran by the land of Zarahemla." (Alma 2:15.) That this river flowed at some point in a north-south direction is implied by such statements as that Alma went "over upon the east of the river Sidon" (Alma 6:7) and "on the west of the river Sidon . . . by the borders of the wilderness" (Alma 8:3). Since it ran through at least part of the South Wilderness (see Alma 16:6), which was east of the land of Zarahemla, it must have "run by" (i.e., been part of or near) the eastern rather than the western borders of Zarahemla. (Clearly the western boundary of the land of Zarahemla, as of the adjoining land of Bountiful (Alma 63:5), was the western seacoast.)

Alma 22:29 states: "And . . . the Nephites had taken possession of all the northern parts of the land bordering on the wilderness, at the head of the river Sidon, from the east to the west, round about on the wilderness side; on the north, even until they came to the land which they called Bountiful." This implies that the head of the river Sidon was somewhere south of Bountiful.

The record makes no mention of the Sidon running by the land of Bountiful, nor of its flowing near the land of Nephi-Lehi. Presumably therefore it sprang forth from its headwaters either on the southern borders of Bountiful or somewhat south of that in Zarahemla. Book of Mormon references already quoted suggest that it flowed southward along or near the border of the land of Zarahemla, then turned eastward through the South Wilderness and made its way to the Sea East.

Sea South, Sea North, Sea East, Sea West

"And it came to pass that they did multiply and spread, and did go forth from the land southward to the land northward, and did spread insomuch that they began to cover the face of the whole earth, from the sea south to the sea north, from the sea west to the sea east." (Helaman 3:8.) These are the names the record gives to the seas which completely surrounded the "isle of the sea" (2 Nephi 10:20) that comprised the land northward and the land southward.

Cumorah

The record says that around A.D. 327 Mormon's armies "began to retreat towards the north countries." (Mormon 2:3.) Later they were still being driven northward. (Mormon 2:20.) In about A.D. 350 Mormon noted: "And the Lamanites did give unto us the land northward, yea, even to the narrow passage which led to the land southward. And we did give unto the Lamanites all the land southward." (Mormon 2:29.) With the Lamanite pressure continually thrusting northward, the statement that the Nephites "did march forth to the land of Cumorah" (Mormon 6:4) clearly puts Cumorah many miles north of the narrow neck of land.

Part I
Isle or Continent

Chimu jug (Peru)

CHAPTER 1

Isle or Continent

Book of Mormon geography is fascinating yet mysterious. For many years students of that book have spent endless hours studying potsherds, archaeological remains, old and new maps, and the terrain of both Central and South America. Yet, lacking the essential breakthrough of knowledge, no one has been able to establish the basic geographical setting which must precede the identifying of the lands and cities of the Nephites and the Jaredites. I believe that breakthrough has now been made, as outlined in this chapter.

Isle of the Sea

As we give careful attention to the geographical details provided in the Book of Mormon itself we must not overlook an important clue. The clue was given to us by Jacob, the brother of Nephi, when he said: ". . . for we are not cast off; nevertheless, we have been driven out of the land of our inheritance; but we have been led to a better land, for the Lord has made the sea our path, and *we are upon an isle of the sea.*" (2 Nephi 10:20. Italics added.)

It may well be asked, Did Jacob really know that his people were upon an isle of the sea rather than a continent? His next words seem to indicate that he did: "But great are the promises of the Lord unto them who are upon the isles of the sea; wherefore as it says isles, there must needs be more than this [island], and they are inhabited also by our brethren." (2 Nephi 10:21.) Furthermore the Nephites had been upon their island perhaps thirty years at this point; had trekked inland from the original west coast landing-point (see chapter 5); and perhaps knew through exploration the distance from their land to the east coast.

According to Joseph Smith, the Nephites inhabited the American continents. Yet in what part of this immense land is the Nephite Island of which Jacob spoke? Look at a map. By no stretch of the imagination could North or South America, as we now know it, be classified as an "isle of the sea."

In the two and a half millennia since Nephi recorded Jacob's words the Nephite Island has changed beyond recognition. But there are surprises in store for those who will look closely at a map of South America. Look with the thought of an island in your mind's eye. Notice the relatively small area occupied by the Andes mountain range. Might that range have constituted our Nephite Island? Let us suppose that *the Amazon basin was then a fresh-water sea and that what is now Argentina was completely inundated.* Given this supposition, our evasive "isle of the sea" emerges.

East Sea

It is my conviction that this represents the great breakthrough in Book of Mormon geography, the hitherto unrecognized factor which defines not only the Nephite "isle of the sea" but also (as we shall see later) that other vital point of reference "the narrow neck of land." For as this chapter will show, the Amazon "sea" is not a supposition. There is ample evidence that it existed.

The 1971 edition of the *Encyclopaedia Britannica* reports that at one time "the Amazon valley was occupied by a great

fresh-water sea. . . ."[1] Dr. James J. Parsons, Professor of Geography at the University of California at Berkeley, confirms that ". . . fossils indicate that a sea occupied the basin. . . ."[2] Even today the basin or flood plain is very low. At the Peru-Brazil border it is only 213 feet above sea level.[3] More than two hundred large rivers feed into the basin from surrounding mountains. This drainage system covers a total area of 2,722,000 square miles.[4] Apparently in the days of Nephi it kept the East Sea full. Today it keeps the mighty Amazon flowing.

The Amazon is four or five miles wide in most places.[5] Some sections reach a width of seven miles. During the month of June, flooding occurs a thousand miles from the mouth, causing the river to widen in some places up to four hundred miles.[6] Below Manaus, Brazil, the river has a depth of no less than seventy-five feet and at the Obidos narrows it exceeds two hundred feet in depth.[7]

The main tributary of the Amazon is the Marañon. Its headwaters are located high in the west central Peruvian Andes, about a hundred miles from the Pacific Ocean. At first the Marañon flows northward toward the northern boundaries of Peru. It then makes a sharp bend eastward to empty itself into the Amazon river valley far below.

The meaning of the Spanish word *marañon* is interesting to our purpose. It means "sea or not." The name was given to the river when it was discovered by Orellana, a Spanish conquistadore and co-adventurer with Pizarro. Orellana had left the company of Pizarro with sixty others in search of

---

[1]Orland Emile White et al., "Amazon," *Encyclopaedia Britannica*, 1971, vol. 1, p. 712.

[2]From a letter to me dated May 20, 1971, from Professor James J. Parsons of the University of California, Berkeley.

[3]William Benton (publisher), "Amazon River, South America," *Britannica Junior*, (Encyclopaedia Britannica, Inc., 1960), vol. 2, p. 212.

[4]White et al., *Britannica*, p. 710.

[5]Dr. R. Kay Gresswell and Anthony Huxley (eds.), "Amazon," *Standard Encyclopedia of the World's Rivers and Lakes* (New York: G. P. Putnam's Sons, 1965), p. 33.

[6]A. Merriam-Webster, *Webster's New Geographical Dictionary* (Springfield, Mass.: G. and C. Merriam Co., 1972), p. 42.

[7]Gresswell and Huxley, *Rivers and Lakes*, p. 33.

food. He had expected eventually to reach the sea by following the Rio Napo down the east side of the Andes. When the Napo reached and merged with the great waters of the Marañon his companions exclaimed, "Is this the sea or not?" The enormous volume of water coming together at the river junction must have had the appearance of a sea — but there was some doubt. Thus, it became known as the "Marañon" — "sea or not."[8]

The Amazon itself has been known by many like names, for instance, the "Sweet Sea" and the "Freshwater Sea." Kempton E. Webb of Columbia University has said that from the air "the Amazon does not look like an ordinary river. It looks more like a great river-sea. . . ."[9] Willard Price, in his book *The Amazing Amazon,* tells us that the Amazon has all the characteristics of a sea.[10] And little wonder, for it once was a sea!

East Sea South

To satisfy the requirements of the "isle of the sea," the Andean coastline of our original supposition must have extended much further south even than the vast Amazon basin. What is the evidence for a sea in that area, the Nephites' East Sea south?

For this evidence we go to an otherwise unlikely ally — Charles Darwin. Unmistakable evidences found by Darwin on his voyage of the *Beagle* to South America (1834-35) confirm that Argentina indeed was completely inundated at one time, as also were Uruguay, Paraguay, and the southern half of Chile. By consulting the map on page 11 you can follow the evidence as it is outlined below and its implications for our "isle of the sea."

Darwin made his first discovery significant to our purpose along the Atlantic coast of Patagonia (lower Argentina). There he found white beds of sea shells including giant oyster

---
[8]Adapted from Willard Price, *The Amazing Amazon* (New York: The John Day Company, 1952), p. 42.
[9]Kempton E. Webb, "Amazon River," *Encyclopedia Americana,* 1971, vol. 1, p. 657.
[10]Price, *Amazing Amazon,* p. 10.

shells, some of which measured twelve inches in diameter. Over these were scattered small stones resembling pumice. These beds averaged two hundred miles in breadth and about fifty feet in thickness.[11] This indicated to Darwin that "everything in this southern continent has been effected on a grand scale: The land, from Rio Plata [Argentina] to Tierra del Fuego [the southern tip of South America], a distance of 1,200 miles, has been raised in mass . . . within the period of the now existing seashells."[12] That is to say, that entire land was once under water.

After making this startling observation Darwin moved over to the Chilean coast (Pacific side). He made a trip to the foot of the Andes for the purpose of seeing ". . . great beds of shells, which stand . . . above the level of the sea and are burnt for lime."[13] He found these shells near Valparáiso, not many miles from today's Santiago and 160 miles north of Talca,[14] some of them on beaches 1,300 feet higher than the present beach. Some were embedded in a "reddish-black" vegetable mold which was found to be "marine mud." Darwin summed up by saying, "The proofs of the elevation of this whole line of coast are unequivocal."[15]

Following his observations of the coast he traveled from Santiago, Chile, over the Andes by way of the Portillo pass to Mendoza, Argentina. He recorded that a few miles north of Mendoza, ". . . at an elevation of about seven thousand feet, I observed on a bare slope some snow-white projecting columns. These were petrified trees, eleven being silicified [petrified with silica], and from thirty to forty converted into coarsely crystallized white calcareous spar [chalkstone]. . . . It required little geological practice to interpret the marvelous story which this scene at once unfolded; though I confess I was at first so much astonished, that I could scarcely believe

---

[11]Charles Darwin, *Voyage of the Beagle* (London: J. M. Dent and Sons, 1906), pp. 162-163.
[12]Darwin, *Beagle,* pp. 162-163.
[13]Darwin, *Beagle,* p. 242.
[14]Only the high beaches near Valparáiso seemed to have been submerged. Indications are that the Nephite Island ended near Talca, Chile, about 1,300 miles north of Tierra del Fuego. See section on Inca roads, chapter 5.
[15]Darwin, *Beagle,* p. 242.

the plainest evidence. I saw the spot where a cluster of fine trees once waved their branches on the shores of the Atlantic when that ocean (now driven back 700 miles) came to the foot of the Andes. . . ."[16]

We may now turn to evidences which show that this sea completely covered today's Uruguay, Argentina and Paraguay. Darwin explored the Argentina-Uruguayan pampas (a vast, extremely flat, treeless plain) as he moved northward along the Parana river from Buenos Aires to Santa Fe. Near Santa Fe he found ". . . beds containing sharks' teeth and sea-shells. . . ,"[17] indicating that the sea had once reached northward at least as far as Santa Fe.

It is interesting to note that even today during the rainy season flooding occurs over the pampas for thousands of square miles, leaving in its wake vast swamps.

Earl Parker Hanson, Chairman, Department of Geography and Geology of the University of Delaware from 1949-1956, believes that the *Gran Chaco Boreal,* a plain covering the western section of Paraguay and the northwestern section of Argentina, was ". . . at one time the bed of an ancient sea. . . ."[18] In reference to that belief, Professor Butland of the University of New England, Armidale, Australia, has said in a letter to me: "There is little doubt whatever that a considerable area of the plains of South America, between the Andes and the Brazilian plat-au [sic] were geosynclinal [having a great downward folding of the earth crust] . . . although . . . most of the Chaco is comparatively unknown, the general nature of the sediments consists of clays, sands, and mudstones for a considerable depth . . . eastward flowing rivers can be considered as the continuing deposition [deposit] on a filled-up gulf. As I indicated above, details of the sedimentary geology are remarkably scarce but I have little doubt that the fossiliferous remains in the strata of the Chaco would support the above theory."[19]

---

[16]Darwin, *Beagle,* pp. 318-319.
[17]Darwin, *Beagle,* p. 122.
[18]Earl Parker Hanson and Gilbert James Butland, "Paraguay," *Encyclopaedia Britannica,* 1973, vol. 17, p. 306.
[19]From a letter to me dated July 20, 1971, from Professor Gilbert James Butland of the University of New England, Armidale, Australia.

It appears then that, covering both the pampas and the Gran Chaco Boreal, this great bay or arm of the sea reached inland to as far as the continental divide — a land barrier which divides today's Amazon basin from the Chaco. This divide was probably slightly lower then and, no doubt continuously flooded by an overflow from the East (Amazon) Sea.

The evidence so far presented is shown in map form on page 17, the western island there being the Nephite/Lamanite one of Book of Mormon times. The distance from the Plata estuary to the continental divide is over one thousand miles. This great bay or gulf would have formed the Nephite East Sea south which, with the East Sea of the Amazon basin, separated the west island from the east island.

East Island

As to the east island, there is a probable reference to it in pre-Christian times. "The historian Plutarch . . . recorded the yarn of certain sailors who landed in Spain about 60 B.C. after visiting, so they said, two large Atlantic islands 10,000 stadia (about 1,200 miles) west of the African coast."[20] ". . . The distance between the eastern part of Brazil . . . and Freetown, Sierra Leone, on the west coast of Africa, is only 1,632 miles."[21] It would seem that these sailors were referring to the South American Continent as it appeared B.C. and as our map "Probable Geophysical Configuration of South America Before the Time of Christ" now reconstructs it.

An inscribed stone, reportedly found on the banks of the Paraiba river, about a hundred miles north of Rio de Janeiro, Brazil, calls that area (B.C.) *Iron Island.*[22] Cyrus H. Gordon, Professor of Mediterranean Studies, Brandeis University, author of the book *Before Columbus,* translated the inscription as follows:

---

[20]Robert Larson, "Was America the Wonderful Land of Fusang?" *American Heritage* (April 1966), p. 43.

[21]Benton, "South America," *Britannica Junior,* vol. 13, p. 404.

[22]There are two Paraiba rivers in Brazil; one is located about one hundred miles north of Rio de Janeiro, the other is where the continent reaches farthest east. Dr. Gordon said that the Paraiba nearest Rio de Janeiro has iron deposits in the vicinity.

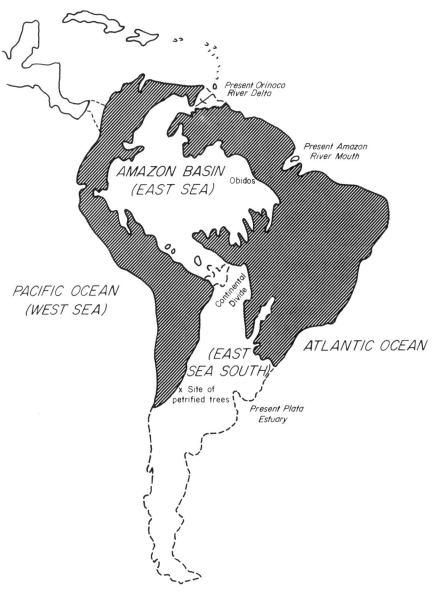

PROBABLE GEOPHYSICAL CONFIGURATION
OF SOUTH AMERICA
BEFORE THE TIME OF CHRIST

"We are Sidonian Canaanites from the city of the Merchant King. We were cast up on this distant island, a land of mountains. We sacrificed a youth to the celestial gods and goddesses in the 19th year of our mighty King Hiram and embarked from Ezion-geber into the Red Sea. We voyaged with ten ships and were at sea together for two years around Africa. Then we were separated by the hand of Baal and were no longer with our companions. So we have come here, 12 men and three women, into 'Island of Iron.' Am I, the admiral, a man who would flee? Nay! May the celestial gods and goddesses favor us well."

Twice this inscription refers to the area as an island, once as a distant island and again as "Island of Iron." This confirms that there was indeed an island where Brazil stands today. We shall call that island the East Island.

Looming high on the west was our Nephite Island, which stretched from today's Colombia to central Chile. The East Island, not so high as the west or Nephite Island, must have extended from the Orinoco river to today's Uruguay, forming an unbroken rim or dam on the east side of the East Sea. It would appear that the catastrophic upheavals at the time of Christ changed the elevation of the land, from the Guiana highlands (on the north) to the Brazilian highlands (on the south). It would also appear that they caused a section of those highlands to crumble and wash away. Today the Amazon river flows through this break in the highlands. No longer are there two large islands, for the face of the land has changed (3 Nephi 8:12), and one large continent remains.

Drainage

The Orinoco river spills into the Atlantic Ocean a little south of the island of Trinidad. It has developed a large delta covering 7,700 square miles and extending 100 miles from its original mouth into the Atlantic Ocean.[23] This com-

---

[23]Gresswell and Huxley, *Rivers and Lakes*, p. 200.

pares with the Nile river, which similarly has a delta extending 100 miles from the original Egyptian shoreline.[24]

The Amazon river outlet contrasts greatly with both the Nile and the Orinoco deltas. Though the Amazon dumps great loads of sediment (1,500,000 tons per day)[25] into the Atlantic Ocean, it has failed to build a sizable delta. Clearly this is because the Amazon has not been flowing long enough to form a substantial delta. The size of the Orinoco delta, on the other hand, indicates that it was once the main outlet to the Nephite East Sea.

Today the Amazon flows through a six-thousand-foot breakthrough at Obidos, five hundred miles from the Amazon's mouth. The mountain stumps on either side of the Obidos narrows suggest that there was indeed a breakthrough at that point. This appears to be consistent with the views of Dr. Gresswell and Anthony Huxley who suggest that "with the rise of the Andes in the west [Chilean uplift], there has in fact been some downward tilting of the continent toward the east. . . ."[26]

A large enough downward shifting of the continent eastward would have placed enough pressure against the Obidos bank to collapse it. The evidence suggests that this is what happened. Taking the evidence in this chapter with all the rest that is presented in this book, it is my opinion that this breakthrough took place at the time of the crucifixion of Christ, when ". . . the whole face of the land was changed. . . ." (3 Nephi 8:12.) Up to that time the main East Sea outlet had been what is now the mouth of the Orinoco river. With the land tilt and the breakthrough at Obidos the East Sea drained, as did the land to the south formerly covered by water, and the result was the configuration of the South American continent as we know it today.

Nephite Island Established

The conclusion is that Jacob knew whereof he spoke when he referred to the Nephite "isle of the sea." The evi-

---

[24]Boris Arnov, Jr., *Secret of Inland Waters* (Boston: Little, Brown and Co., 1965), p. 64.
[25]White et al., *Britannica*, p. 712.
[26]Gresswell and Huxley, *Rivers and Lakes*, p. 33.

dence presented in the present chapter indicates within reasonably close limits the coastline of that island, as shown in the accompanying map. Having arrived at this basic definition of the territory involved, we can now proceed to locate on the map some of the geographical features referred to in the Book of Mormon.

Part II
The Land Northward

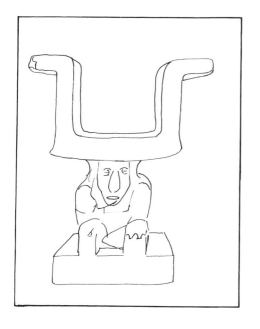

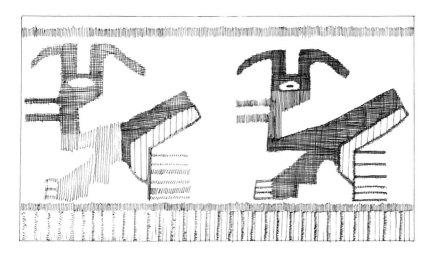

Textile design (Peru)

CHAPTER 2
The Narrow Neck

The Narrow Neck

As every student of the Book of Mormon knows, and as our Introduction briefly points out, the "narrow neck" of land so frequently referred to in the sacred record is a major key to Book of Mormon geography. The basic relationships between that land bridge and the land northward on the one hand, and the land southward on the other, are so clearly set out that to establish the identity of that neck, to locate it on a modern map, would be to have the over-all picture of the Book of Mormon lands fall immediately into place. Thus any attempt to portray Book of Mormon geography on a modern map had best start with the narrow neck of land.

When we look at a modern map, the most immediately attractive choice for the narrow neck is the Isthmus of Darien (Panama). The short distance across its most narrow point would even seem to meet one of the stated conditions for the narrow neck. (See Alma 22:32.) Indeed, if we were confined to the modern map, it is difficult to see where else the selection could fall but somewhere along the isthmus of Central America.

But there are stronger reasons for rejecting that area than for selecting it. So far as the eastern half of the Isthmus of Darien (Panama) is concerned, one reason is the absence of civilized remains. A. Hyatt Verrill, in his book *Old Civilizations of the New World,* describes the 150-mile stretch between Colombia and Central Panama (Darien Gap) as being "another mystery which no one can solve . . ." for, says he, that land "appears absolutely barren of all signs of occupation by civilized or even highly cultured tribes."[1]

If Panama were the Book of Mormon's narrow neck of land, as has generally been accepted, it is difficult to understand why no traces of the Nephite people have been found scattered along this "gap." The absence of such traces would seem to confirm the conclusion of Carleton Beals that Panama (at least part of it) previously was submerged and ". . . the [South American] continent isolated."[2] This places the narrow neck of land elsewhere.

Some have concluded that the narrow neck of land must have been the Isthmus of Tehuantepec in Mexico. But again, apart from its being rather too wide to fit the conditions of Alma 22:32, both this isthmus and the Isthmus of Darien (Panama) appear to be ruled out by Alma 50:34 which says: "And it came to pass that they did not head them until they had come to the borders of the land Desolation; and there they did head them, by the narrow pass which led by the sea into the land northward, yea, by the sea, on the west and on the east." This verse and Alma 22:32, taken together, make clear that the narrow passage was on the narrow neck of land separating the land southward from the land northward. Notice that the narrow pass led by the sea *on the west* and *on the east.*

The two isthmuses are reproduced as part of the accompanying map. Looking at it in relation to Alma 50:34, one

---

[1] A. Hyatt Verrill, *Old Civilizations of the New World,* copyright 1929, 1956 (Indianapolis: The Bobbs-Merrill Company, Inc.), p. 48. Used with permission.

[2] Carleton Beals, *Nomads and Empire Builders* (Philadelphia: The Chilton Book Company, 1961), p. 39.

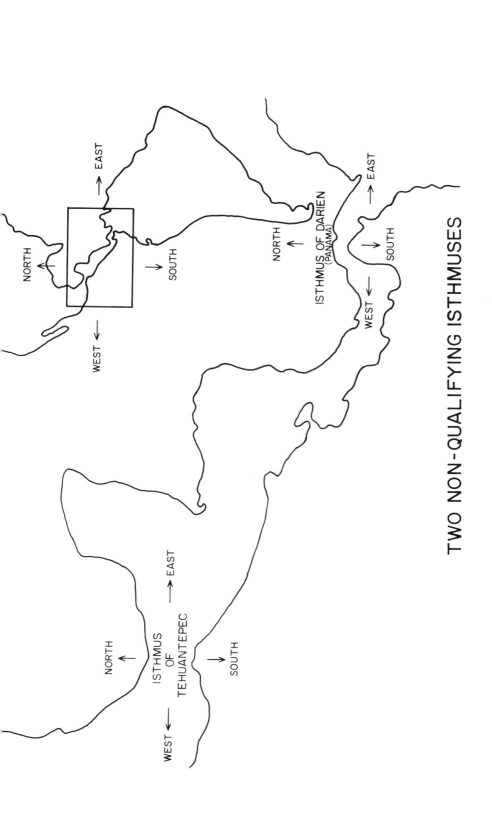

TWO NON-QUALIFYING ISTHMUSES

might ask, "To a person traveling across a narrow pass on the Isthmus of Tehuantepec or the Isthmus of Darien (Panama) today, would the sea be on the east and on the west or would it be on the north and on the south?" Clearly in both cases the sea would be on the north and on the south. This seems to be a compelling reason to eliminate both the Isthmus of Darien and the Isthmus of Tehuantepec in our search for the narrow neck of land.

According to the Book of Ether the narrow neck was ". . . by the place where the sea divides the land." (Ether 10:20.) Apparently this meant that the sea swept inland and formed a gulf. The word "neck" seems to imply that this gulf was elongated, forming a shoreline along an isthmus.

Since the Nephite landing took place on the west coast of South America (our west island of chapter 1), and since the narrow neck is referred to long before the mention of ships (Alma 63:5-8) which might have overcome the "isolation" caused by the submerged "Darien Gap," we would expect to look for the elongated gulf on the Pacific coast of South America. The only such geographical location along that coast is the Gulf of Guayaquil in southern Ecuador. Apparently then this yawning eighty- to a-hundred-mile gulf once shaped the western shoreline of the Book of Mormon's narrow neck of land. With this established we may begin to look for the eastern shoreline of the isthmus.

Eastward of the Gulf of Guayaquil is the irregular and deeply broken Loja valley at a height of 7,300 feet.[3] Of all the Andes topography, Loja has the easiest entrance into the Amazon, our proposed Nephite East Sea. One need only follow the Rio Zamora down the east side of the Andes in order to reach the upper Amazon basin.[4]

---

[3]Loja has a subtropical climate. It is the home of the magical powder, quinine. It would appear that the Nephites knew of the fever-bark tree. (See Alma 46:40.)

[4]Today the Zamora river trail down the east side of the Andes, like the Cuenca trail, is arduous and steep. Heavy rain (sometimes as much as two hundred inches a year) falls upon the eastern side of the Cordillera Oriental. The eastern side of the Cordillera Oriental reflects the tropical rain forest conditions which prevail to as far as 10° latitude both north and south of the equator. These conditions would have naturally been the same since the days of the

It is difficult to say how high the water level rose above the base of the Andes in ancient times.[5] No doubt it was sufficiently high for the East Sea to "back-fill" into the lower reaches (perhaps even the upper reaches) of the Zamora river gorge. This sea-filled gorge would have partially formed the eastern shores of the narrow neck, as also would that of the Upano river. (See accompanying map, "The Narrow Neck of Land.")

"And now, it was only the distance of a day and a half's journey for a Nephite, on the line Bountiful and the land Desolation, from the east to the west sea; and thus the land of Nephi and the land of Zarahemla were nearly surrounded by water, there being a small neck of land between the land northward and the land southward." (Alma 22:32.)

It appears from the above evidence that "the distance of a day and a half's journey . . . from the east to the west sea" began at Loja, a point in the eastern Andes very close to the East Sea. Strengthening this conclusion is the fact that in ancient times the Inca road ran from Cuzco (Peru) through Loja to Quito, which again suggests Loja as the eastern point in the Nephites' narrow neck of land.

The distance from Loja and the upper Zamora river to the Gulf of Guayaquil is about seventy-five miles. Modern historians know that Inca long-distance relay runners carried fresh fish two hundred miles inland from the coast in two days' time.[6] Clearly a Nephite runner would have been able to cover the distance from Loja to the Gulf of Guayaquil in "a day and a half's journey."

Knowing the approximate width of the narrow neck on its southern border leads to the question of how far north the narrow neck extended. About 120 miles north of Loja, at a point east and north of Cuenca, there is a lookout point (11,490 feet). Here the slopes fall off and one can see the steaming Amazon jungles below. In the days of the Nephites

---

Jaredites, even though there may have been some remarkable changes in the elevation of the land.

[5]Today, along the base of the Andes the run-off is so poor as to leave waist-deep slime.

[6]Victor Wolfgang von Hagen, *Highway of the Sun* (New York: Duell, Sloan and Pearce, Inc. with Little, Brown and Co., 1955), pp. 241, 242.

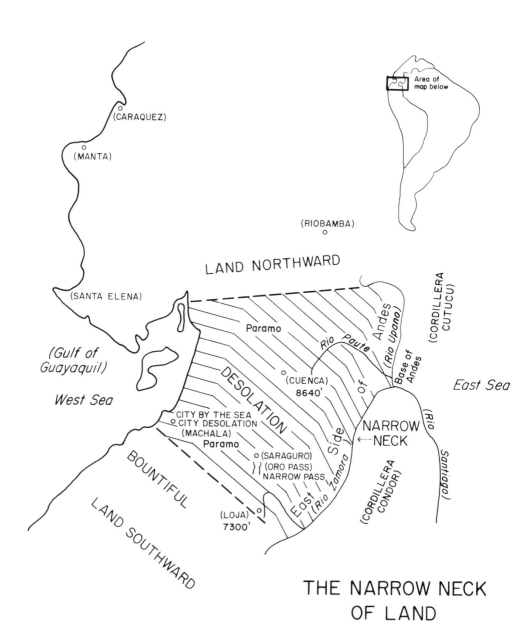

and the Jaredites the blue of the East Sea would have been seen from this point. Presumably it was here that the narrow neck ended, the width on its northern borders, from the lookout point to the Gulf of Guayaquil, being about a hundred miles.

Thus evidence indicates that the narrow neck was that land which lies between the Gulf of Guayaquil and the upper Amazon basin.

Narrow Pass or Passage

Another important landmark associated with the narrow neck of land requires attention here. We often hear the terms *narrow neck of land* and *narrow pass* or *narrow passage* used synonymously; and understandably so, for the Book of Mormon wording makes the two inseparable. Even so, a narrow neck of land, if viewed correctly, is an isthmus. A narrow pass or passage is more often than not a defile or gorge between mountains, or in other words a mountain pass. In references before the visits of Christ the Book of Mormon uses the term *narrow or small neck of land,* but it does not use the term after that. (Alma 63:5; Alma 22:32; Ether 10:20.) On the other hand, the narrow pass or passage is spoken of both before and after the time of Christ. This tells us that the narrow pass or passage remained after the great destruction. (Before Christ — Alma 50:34; 52:9. After Christ — Mormon 2:29; 3:5.) Clearly the narrow pass or passage was located on the narrow neck of land, but where?

North of Loja and south of Saraguro there is a high and narrow pass called "El Paso del Oro." It is an important pass, one which in early days had a way of controlling movement between Peru and Ecuador. In the days of the conquistadores a battle called "La Batalla del Oro" was fought to conquer that pass. When we recognize the location of this pass in connection with the narrow neck of land it is easy to see why the two terms have been used synonymously.

Desolation

". . . Desolation [reached] . . . so far northward that it came into the land which had been peopled and been destroyed, of whose bones we have spoken. . . ." (Alma 22:30.)

It is clear that the land "which had been peopled and been destroyed," the land of the Jaredites, was the land northward, as the Book of Ether indicates. The writer of that book as we now have it was Moroni, who bridged the two civilizations in his usage of Nephite geographical terms when portraying the Jaredite story. Thus he tells how Jaredite flocks ". . . began to flee before the poisonous serpents, towards the land southward . . ." and that some "fled into the land southward." (Ether 9:31-32.) Likewise, having "built a great city by the narrow neck of land . . . they did preserve the land southward for a wilderness, to get game." (Ether 10:20-21.)

". . . Bountiful . . . bordered upon the land which they called Desolation. . . ." (Alma 22:29-30.) As we saw in the Introduction, Bountiful was in the northernmost part of the land southward. Clearly then, Desolation must have been another name for what was otherwise known as the narrow neck of land or a part of it. It would seem too that Desolation was included, at least sometimes, in references to the land northward; for example, as follows: ". . . the Nephites possessing all the land northward, yea, even all the land which was northward of the land Bountiful, according to their pleasure." (Alma 50:11.)

That stretch of land called Desolation by the Nephites is vividly described by Victor von Hagen when he says that "twisted lava . . . [alternating] with gaping craters"[7] is the topography. Between the saucer-shaped valleys of Loja and Cuenca and also north of Cuenca are flat, bleak, treeless plateaus called paramos. The paramos are very cold. Bitter, arctic, hail-packed gales on these plateaus have sent countless travelers to the grave. Others have been knocked senseless there by sudden hailstorms.[8]

Even so, cities were built on the land Desolation. (Mormon 4.) Some were in the high Andean valleys such as

---

[7] Victor Wolfgang von Hagen, *Ecuador and the Galapagos Islands* (University of Oklahoma Press, 1949), p. 65.

[8] Von Hagen, *Ecuador and the Galapagos*, pp. 65, 66.

Cuenca, where traces of an ancient stone city and the Inca road may be found. Others were along the seashore, where the homes were probably constructed of reeds. We find that the Jaredites ". . . built a great city by the narrow neck . . . by the place where the sea divides the land." (Ether 10:20.) In all probability this city was near today's Machala, Ecuador.

Machala can easily be reached today by taking a boat from the mouth of the Guayas river across the Gulf of Guayaquil to the natural port of Puerto Bolivar.[9] Rich jungle grows thickly along the shores. Machala is about two miles northeast of its port, Puerto Bolivar.

Although the Jaredites built a city by the narrow neck, they seem to have shown little interest in extending their cultivated lands further south. Again, the Book of Ether tells us that ". . . they did preserve the land southward for a wilderness, to get game." (Ether 10:21.)

In the high Andes south of Loja the land consists of peaks, mountain knots, canyons and narrow valleys. This difficult terrain stretches from Loja, Ecuador, to Cajamarca, Peru, a distance of over two hundred miles, and would have acted as a barrier against too much movement from the land northward into the land southward. South of the Gulf of Guayaquil, along the Peruvian coast, the land is a sandy waste. Rain falls on this desert on only very rare occasions. Small wonder, then, that the Jaredites did not extend their lands further south.[10]

Many years after the Jaredites built their city by the sea, the people of Nephi moved out onto the narrow neck and also built a city by the sea. They called their city Desolation. "And . . . the Lamanites did come down [meaning out of the Andes to the coast] to the city of Desolation to battle . . .

---

[9]In the days of the Jaredites probably balsa log rafts were used.

[10]One word of explanation should be given concerning lands. When a Nephite used the expression "the land" or "the land of" he usually spoke of a city with its surrounding agricultural lands. Sometimes "the land of" referred to larger areas similar to our counties of today. These areas included within their boundaries several cities with their agricultural lands. For example, the land of Zarahemla included the city Zarahemla, the city Gideon, the city Jershon, and more. Sometimes even larger areas were referred to as "the land." These were land tracts such as "the land northward" and "the land southward."

and . . . we did beat them . . . and did slay a great number of them, and their dead were cast into the sea." (Mormon 3:7-8.)[11]

Desolation, then, included the city Desolation with its surrounding lands on the Gulf of Guayaquil, the Andean valleys with their cities and lands, and the paramos.

---

[11]The sudden change in the altitude, from above 7,000 feet to sea level, would affect the fighting ability of an army. The same thing would be true if an army moved from sea level to over 7,000 feet.

Slant-eyed, pre-Columbian bust (Ecuador)

CHAPTER 3
Jaredite Lands

The Jaredite Landing

Book of Mormon passages such as Ether 9:31-33 and 10:20-21 indicate that the Jaredite nation occupied "the land northward," that land "which was northward of the land Bountiful" (Alma 50:11). This was the land at and northward of the narrow neck of land, which the previous chapter identifies with the Gulf of Guayaquil on the west and the Andean coastline of the former East Sea on the east. The reasonable conclusion, therefore, is that the Jaredite landing took place on the coast of today's Ecuador, north of Guayaquil.

This conclusion coincides not only with the Book of Mormon but also with incidents recorded by Spanish chroniclers, as told them by ancient record- (quipu) keepers and "rememberers of history." For instance, Philip Ainsworth Means, in his book *Ancient Civilizations of the Andes,* quotes the interpretation of an Inca quipu- or record-keeper named Catari, as follows: "The remote forebears of the Indians were driven to America from the Old World after the Deluge, and eventually some of them reached Caracas, which may possibly be identified with Caráques, on the Ecuadorian coast. ... Others landed at Sampu, called by the Spaniards Santa Elena ... also on the Ecuadorian coast."[1] (See map, "Narrow Neck of Land," chapter 2.)

Following the landing it is safe to say that the Jaredites did not stay on the coast but moved "up unto" mountain lands. The book of Ether records that Jared, his brother, their families and friends "went forth upon the face of the land." (Ether 6:13.) Later, when Corihor rebelled, he had to go "up unto the land of Moron" (Ether 7:5) to get to the seat of government, the area which apparently was thought of as "the land of their first inheritance." (Ether 7:16-17.) On the basis that Ecuador was the place of the Jaredite landing, the words "up unto the land of Moron" would of course mean "up unto" the inter-Andean highlands.

Inter-Andean Highlands

An indication of the terrain and climate of the coastal area is sufficient to understand why the Jaredite people would move "up unto" the land of Moron rather than remain on the coast. Santa Elena, one of the proposed places for the Jaredite landing, is hot and dry. Obtaining sufficient drinking water would have been a problem in this area, especially as the settlement grew. East of Santa Elena, near the chocolate-colored Guayas river, vegetation becomes heavy and water is more easily obtained, but here the continuous heat (averaging about 90° temperatures) and humidity create a perfect climate for hosts of disease-carrying insects. Yellow fever, malaria, and liver fluke are prevalent. Mildew and mold destroy textiles and leather. Termites can, and sometimes do, undermine a wooden structure almost overnight.

The Bay of Caráques or Caráquez, the other proposed Jaredite landing, receives the waters of the Rio Chone. The land stretching southward from the river is semi-desert. Here,

---

[1]Philip A. Means, *Ancient Civilizations of the Andes* (New York: Charles Scribner's Sons, 1931), p. 210.

as at Santa Elena, sufficient drinking water would have been a problem. Immediately north of the Rio Chone the rain forest is dominant, creating climatic conditions similar to that around the Rio Guayas. Thus, living along the coast would have been neither easy nor healthy for the Jaredites.

Eastward from the coast an unusual change in elevation and topography produces a very different climatic picture. For the full length of Ecuador two massive mountain ranges run parallel in a north-south direction. Between these mountain ranges — Cordillera Occidental (west) and Cordillera Oriental (east) — is a plain or plateau measuring about two hundred miles in length, varying from nineteen to thirty miles in width, and ranging from eight thousand to more than nine thousand feet in height. This plain or plateau is divided by a few mountain spurs, leaving several shallow basins or plains where the climate is healthy and where three-fourths of the population of modern Ecuador live. On the northern end of this inter-Andean plain, almost exactly on the equator, is the 9,300-foot Quito valley. Cuenca, at 8,640 feet, lies at the southern end of the plain. The Incas, it is said, called Cuenca the flowering plain.[2] (See map, "Inter-Andean Highlands.")

Moron

Moron, with its surrounding lands, comprised the first "capital" of the Jaredites or the land of their first inheritance. (Ether 7:16-17.) "The land of Moron . . . was near the land which is called Desolation by the Nephites" (Ether 7:6), the land immediately north of the land of Bountiful and therefore comprising the narrow neck of land. (Alma 22:29-31.)

North of the Gulf of Guayaquil, our "narrow neck," near Riobamba (Chimborazo Province), in the central plains of Ecuador, are the ruins of a very old city.[3] These ruins are located about 110 miles south of Quito and about 20 miles southeast of the highest point in Ecuador, Mount Chimborazo. (See map, "Inter-Andean Highlands.") Accord-

---
[2]Von Hagen, *Ecuador and the Galapagos,* p. 70.
[3]Leon E. Seltzer (ed.), *The Columbia Lippincott Gazetteer of the World* (New York: Columbia University Press, 1962), p. 1583.

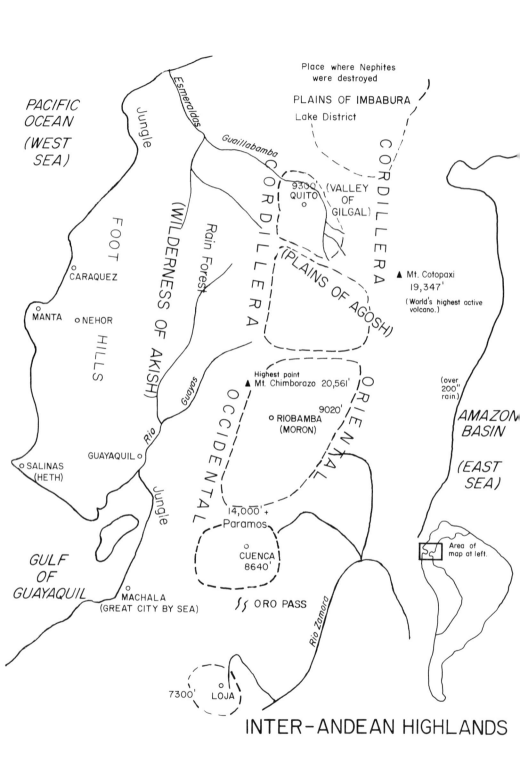

ing to archaeologists they are pre-Inca.[4] Not much remains. Absolutely nothing is left of their buildings, which suggests that their houses were fashioned out of timber.[5]

The book of Helaman speaks of migrations into the land northward, parts of which had been ". . . rendered desolate and without timber, because of the many inhabitants who had before inherited the land." (Helaman 3:5.) It is observed too that, during the final stages of the Jaredite wars, "Shiz pursued after Coriantumr . . . and he did burn the cities." (Ether 14:17.) It seems reasonable then that the only tangible traces of the Jaredite people would have been pottery fragments, metal works, and other such durable evidences. In fact, it is such remains of the Ecuadorian pre-Incas that have been found. Pre-Inca pottery in Ecuador has been dated at about 3,000 B.C.,[6] though our Bible/Book of Mormon chronology would suggest a somewhat later date. This early pottery has been discovered from near Ambato to Cañar (a few miles north of Cuenca) in the highlands, and at Manabi and Guayas on the coast.[7] (See map, "Omer's Journey" for locations.)

Thus the evidence suggests that the Jaredite city of Moron was in the highlands near the site of the modern city of Riobamba.

Nehor

Next to Moron, Nehor is the most important land in Jaredite history. It is first mentioned in connection with Corihor's rebellion against his father, the king at Moron. Corihor, it is said, "went over and dwelt in the land of Nehor."

---

[4]Riobamba not only rated high with the pre-Incas, but also with the Incas and the Spaniards. The Incas, it is said, built a sun temple there, and a royal tambo, while the Spaniards thought of founding their capital at Riobamba.

The word *Inca* means ruler, emperor, or king. It was a title conferred upon each new ruler or king. This may hark back to the succession of kings following Nephi's death, when the people called their ruler "second Nephi, third Nephi, and so forth, according to the reigns of the kings . . . ." (Jacob 1:11.) The word *Inca* now refers to the tribe as well as to the chieftains.

[5]Julian H. Steward (ed.), *Handbook of South American Indians* (New York: Cooper Square Publishers, Inc., 1963), vol. 2, p. 799.

[6]George E. Stuart et al., map, "North America Before Columbus" (Washington, D.C.: National Geographic Society, 1972).

[7]Steward, *Handbook of South American Indians,* vol. 2, p. 772.

(Ether 7:4.) The terms "went over," "came over," and "went up unto" are frequently used in the Book of Mormon to designate a trip into mountain lands from the coast or vice versa. In this case Corihor probably traveled to the foothills of Ecuador, about twenty miles inland from Manta. Scattered throughout that area are the remains of a great civilization which archaeologists have termed the Manabi culture.

According to the experts, the Manabi remains are exceedingly ancient. A. Hyatt and Ruth Verrill said of these people: "Despite the high attainment in art, engineering, astronomy and government which were reached by the Aztecs, the Incas, the Mayas and others, in a way these unknown, forgotten races of South America were more remarkable, and were unquestionably far more ancient. . . ."[8] A. Hyatt Verrill also explains: ". . . it would appear that the Manabis were a distinct race with a culture differing materially from that of any other ancient people of South or Central America."[9]

Corihor stayed at Nehor until he had gained sufficient strength to go "up unto" the land of Moron to battle. (Ether 7:5.) In his attack he overthrew the government at Moron, took his father the king into captivity, and moved the ruling city to Nehor. (Ether 7:5-9.) Many years passed and, although Corihor's father was very old and still in captivity at Nehor, he fathered a son named Shule. (Ether 7:7.)

Corihor continued to rule until his now-grown younger brother Shule relieved him of his stolen kingdom and returned the throne to their father. Because the royal family had been in captivity many years, they naturally would have remained at Nehor. (Ether 7:9-20.) Eventually Shule inherited the kingdom. He too ruled from Nehor. (Ether 7:9-17.) In fact, it appears from the book of Ether that for hundreds of years after Shule the Jaredite people were ruled from Nehor,[10] a fact

---

[8]A. Hyatt Verrill and Ruth Verrill, *America's Ancient Civilizations* (New York: G. P. Putnam's Sons, 1953), p. 148.

[9]A. Hyatt Verrill, *Old Civilizations of the New World*, p. 242. Used by permission.

[10]The seat of the government probably did not switch back to Moron until the days of Com. (Ether 10:32.) Com ruled forty-two years over half the kingdom. This was more than sufficient time to establish a kingly city of his own.

which suggests that the Manabi culture and the Jaredite culture could easily have been one and the same.

Other factors strengthen this similarity. For instance, archaeologists say that the Manabi became so expert in the working of gold that they were able to engrave nuggets the size of the head of an ordinary pin. These nuggets "appear to be natural grains. . . . But when viewed through a magnifying-glass they are [found to be] . . . perfectly and beautifully wrought beads . . . others are built up of several almost invisible pieces welded or soldered together. . . ."[11] Likewise, the Jaredite artisans were expert goldsmiths. "Wherefore he [king Riplakish — approximately the tenth king to rule from Nehor] did obtain all his fine work, yea, even his fine gold he did cause to be refined . . . and all manner of fine workmanship he did cause to be wrought in prison. . . ." (Ether 10:7.)

Thrones represent another similarity between the Manabi and the Jaredite cultures. Numerous elaborately sculptured stone seats and huge thrones — some weighing at least half a ton — have been found scattered over a small area of the Manabi district about twenty miles in diameter. All are U-shaped with no back, like the Roman seat. The bases of these seats or thrones are beautifully sculptured to resemble crouching human figures, animals, and birds, which appear to be supporting the seats.[12] These elaborate thrones call to mind the Book of Mormon statement: "And he [Riplakish] did erect him an exceedingly beautiful throne. . . ." (Ether 10:6.) A number of the Manabi thrones are of volcanic rock and ". . . have been found with traces of human remains adhering to the seats [leading to the conclusion] that the bodies of deceased rulers . . . were fastened in a sitting position on the thrones . . . and left to time and the elements."[13]

What better place to do this than in the land of the Jaredites' first inheritance (Moron)? After Com gained control over all of the kingdom he would have remained in that city. Therefore, it is safe to say that, from the time of Com to the final destruction of the Jaredites, the ruling city was at Moron. (Ether 14:6.)

[11] Verrill and Verrill, *America's Ancient Civilizations,* p. 147.

[12] Edgar L. Hewett, *Ancient Andean Life* (Indianapolis: The Bobbs-Merrill Company, Inc., 1967), pp. 217-218.

[13] Verrill and Verrill, *America's Ancient Civilizations,* p. 147.

Traces of the Jaredites have led us from the Gulf of Guayaquil to the inter-Andean plains at Riobamba to an area in the foothills not far from the Pacific coast. We will now consider the remainder of the Jaredite story on the basis of these locations.

During Shule's reign, his nephew Noah conquered the land of the Jaredites' first inheritance (Ether 7:16), or Moron, with its surrounding lands. This created two kingdoms, one among the coastal hills (Nehor) and one in the inter-Andean highlands (Moron).

Not satisfied with his conquest, Noah "gave battle again unto Shule . . . and carried him away captive into Moron." (Ether 7:17.) Shule's sons followed the invaders into the mountain lands, killed Noah, and reinstated Shule in his own kingdom. (Ether 7:18.) Even so, there remained two kingdoms, Shule ruling the coastal kingdom and Noah's son the highland kingdom. (Ether 7:20.) Eventually Shule reunited the Jaredite nation. (Ether 7:22.)

Land of Heth

Shule died and Omer, his righteous son, reigned in his place. Omer's son Jared "rebelled against his father, and came and dwelt in the land of Heth." (Ether 8:2.)

Jared did not "come over" or "go up unto," but he "came and dwelt." This word suggests that he stayed somewhere in the coastal regions.

Looking northward from the Manabi (Nehor) district we find swampy, mosquito-breeding jungles. The land to the south of Manabi is hot and dry, but fishing along the coast is excellent.[14] One need only dip his basket into the sea to catch enough fish for a meal. Often not even that much effort is required, because as the tide moves out fish are trapped in tidal pools. Crabs are frequently seen racing across the sand,

---

[14]These two extremes in climate are caused by the warm Central American and the cold Humboldt currents which meet off Cape San Lorenzo near Manta. Wherever the Central American currents flow, there is heavy rainfall. Where the Humboldt currents prevail, very little rain falls. (Seltzer, *Columbia Lippincott Gazetteer*, p. 1458.)

and brightly colored shellfish are in abundance.[15] Jared reasonably would have chosen this type of environment over the jungles north of Manabi, so we might tentatively place Heth near the modern Salinas. In any event, Jared possessed the land of Heth, keeping his father in captivity there until his brothers defeated his army and rescued Omer. The loss of the kingdom caused Jared great sorrow and he began to plot the murder of his father.

Omer's Journey

"The Lord warned Omer in a dream that he should depart out of the land." (Ether 9:3.) So it was that with his family Omer "traveled many days, and came over and passed by the hill of Shim. . . ." (Ether 9:3.) It would appear that for safety reasons Omer did not follow the usual route Manta-Guayaquil-Quito.[16] Rather it would seem that he marched due east through heavy rain forest to emerge in the inter-Andean highlands near Mount Chimborazo and the modern Ambato. In that case, Omer would have looked to the mighty Mount Chimborazo (a more than 20,000-foot peak) to guide him, as travelers do today. In the early sixteenth century Pedro de Alvarado, Spanish conquistadore and governor of Guatemala, followed a similar route in his desire to conquer Quito. Alvarado marched due east from the coast near Manta, through heavy rain forest on the western flanks of the Andes, and over the sky-high paramo to reach Riobamba, south of Quito. It was a terrible march in which many of his men perished. It took many days. Omer's trek, before he passed by the hill of Shim, lasted "many days." (Ether 9:3.)

---

[15]Dean Hobbs Blanchard, *Ecuador, Crown Jewel of the Andes* (New York: Vantage Press, 1962), p. 114.

[16]In days past it was an eight-day journey on horseback from Guayaquil-Guaranda (near Mount Chimborazo)-Quito. Victor von Hagen said that this route was "the only route to the cordillera and the city of Quito." (*South America Called Them* [New York: Alfred A. Knopf, Inc., 1945].) Later he pointed out another route north of Manta along the Rio Esmeraldas and over the Andes. However, for reasons unknown to the author, the Guayaquil-Quito route was the most popular, at least in the days of the conquistadores. Omer probably traveled somewhere between these two routes.

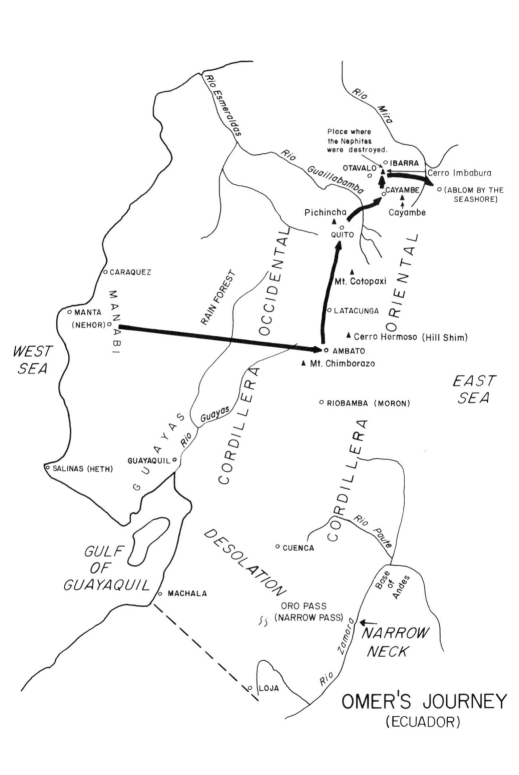

Hill Shim

Omer "came over and passed by the hill of Shim." (Ether 9:3.) Centuries later this was to be an important Nephite hill. Mormon was ten years old when the prophet Ammaron came to him and said, ". . . and when ye are of that age [twenty-four years] go to the land Antum, unto a hill which shall be called Shim; and there have I deposited unto the Lord all the sacred engravings concerning this people." (Mormon 1:3.) Here again, in abridging the Jaredite records, the Nephite Moroni connects the two civilizations geographically, using the "hill of Shim," as he used the land of Cumorah, the "place where the Nephites were destroyed" (Ether 9:3), to show the route Omer traveled.

Though Moroni gave clues as to Omer's route, looking for the hill of Shim in the midst of the Andes mountains would be like looking for the proverbial needle in a haystack. Indian legends and traditions may help, however. The "rememberers of history" were reported as saying that the treasures of the Incas were buried on the slopes of the 15,216-foot cerro Hermoso.[17] In Spanish, *cerro* means *hill* or *high hill*. Cerro Hermoso ("hill beautiful") is about seventeen miles, in a straight line, north-east of Ambato in the Cordillera Oriental or east Andes. If Omer emerged on the central plains near today's Mount Chimborazo and Ambato, and then turned northward to travel along the inter-Andean valley, he undoubtedly passed by today's cerro Hermoso. The Inca "treasure" later buried there, according to the rememberers of history, could easily have been the sacred records which Ammaron buried in the hill of Shim.

Place Where the Nephites Were Destroyed

After Omer passed by the hill of Shim he "came over by the place where the Nephites were destroyed." (Ether 9:3.) From this almost matter-of-fact statement it does not seem unreasonable to conclude that the hill of Shim was no great

---

[17] Andrew Jackson Lamoureux, "Ecuador," *Encyclopaedia Britannica,* 1922, vol. 8, p. 912.

distance from the place "where the Nephites were destroyed." Notice that Omer once again "came over." Since he had already traveled "many days" to arrive at the inter-Andean plains it would be illogical to turn him around and send him westward back to the place from whence he had come. A southward route would have taken him toward the narrow neck of land, an area which Moroni did not mention in connection with Omer's journey. Furthermore the record specifies that Omer went eastward after arriving at the area where the Nephites were destroyed, thus suggesting a change of direction at that point. (Ether 9:3.) The most likely conclusion then is that Omer traveled northward after passing by the hill of Shim.

The wording would indicate that when Omer "came over" he passed over or through a barrier of some kind, such as a high mountain, a deep depression, or some other kind of drastic change in the terrain. While such a barrier is not apparent from an ordinary map of Ecuador, there is such a place. About twelve miles north and east of Quito there is a very deep gorge or canyon called the gorge of Guaillabamba. This gorge extends from the east Andes, through the west Andes, and on out to the Pacific Ocean. Archaeologists say that in times past different cultures tended to form on either side of this great natural obstacle.

Along the level canyon floor flows the Guaillabamba river. Today planes follow the Guaillabamba gorge from the Pacific into Quito. This enables them to reach Quito more easily, as they need not rise to such great heights to cross over the Cordillera Occidental. Assuming that Omer crossed over this abyss, he would have emerged on its northern side near Cayambe. North of Cayambe are the beautiful plains of Imbabura. (See map, "Inter-Andean Highlands.")

Imbabura is Ecuador's lake country and is said to rival the famous lake district of northern England. The names of some of the lakes in Imbabura are: San Pablo (sometimes called Imbacocha), Yaguarcocha, Cuicocha, Cristococha, and Caricocha. There are more. In addition, large rivers flow through this province. They are, to name a few: **Mira,** Chota, Ambi, Itumbe, Llurimagua, Taguando, Chorlavi, and Jatunyacu. The rivers are fed from the run-off of snow in the surrounding mountains and volcano peaks. Imbabura covers an area of about 1,854 square miles. (In comparison, Yellowstone National Park has a total of 2,931 square miles.)

Otavalo, an important town in the province of Imbabura, is forty-two miles from Quito as the crow flies. Over the twisting roads the distance is about seventy miles. Notice that the description of the plains of Imbabura appears to match that of the Book of Mormon land of Cumorah. (See Mormon 6:4.) Further information on Cumorah is contained in chapter 4. (See also the map, "Hill Ramah-Hill Cumorah.")

Omer "came over" by the place where the Nephites were destroyed, which I suggest put him in the plains of Imbabura, and turned eastward to get to Ablom by the seashore.

Ablom by the Seashore

If Imbabura were the land of Cumorah, that would place Ablom by the seashore fairly close to the ruling city of Nehor, perhaps less than 350 miles away — a reasonable distance in the light of later events. Some years after Omer marched out of the land of his inheritance, "a small number of men [who apparently knew the exact location of his exile] . . . fled out of the land, and came over and dwelt with Omer." (Ether 9:9.) Subsequently, after a "space of many years" (Ether 9:12), all the people of the old kingdom were destroyed "save it were thirty souls, and they who fled with the house of Omer. Wherefore, Omer was restored again to the land of his inheritance." (Ether 9:12-13.)

These events indicate that, although Omer had been in exile for many years, he remained in fairly close contact with the people of Nehor. Had he been, say, a thousand miles away from Nehor it is doubtful that he could have maintained such contact or that he would have made the long trek back.

Climatic conditions might suggest other evidence, for a man fleeing for his life might travel and live in unpleasant conditions, while a reprieve would make him look homeward again. Omer "came over by the place where the Nephites were destroyed, and from thence eastward, and came to a place which was called Ablom, by the seashore. . . ." (Ether 9:3.) From the plains of Imbabura, our land of Cumorah, he would have had to travel over the Cordillera Oriental (east Andes) to the shores of the East Sea, a trek of somewhere between twenty and fifty miles. On this route he would with great difficulty pass over the high Cordillera Oriental and then down through the east Andean rain forest. Rain forest suggests poor soils caused by heavy rain which washes away many soluble minerals near the surface, thus limiting agriculture. Additionally, heavy rains create mud slides and shifting jungle. Heavy year-round rain and a constant warm daytime temperature, the climate of the tropical rain forest, make a perfect breeding-ground for insects of all kinds, rodents, and snakes.

It would be difficult to visualize Omer taking his people into such a place had they not been fleeing from murderers. Such conditions would practically guarantee freedom from pursuit. Scattered Indian tribes, such as the Jivaro headhunters, have been able to survive east of the Andes by hunting, fishing, and gathering, and presumably Omer's group would have been tough enough and ingenious enough to do the same. But given such conditions, Omer would have been glad to return when possible to the more pleasant foothills of the Cordillera Occidental (west Andes).

After Omer returned to the land of his inheritance, he lived in relative peace until his death. The people prospered in the land for perhaps two hundred years. Then came the great dearth, bringing with it poisonous serpents.

Poisonous Serpents

"And it came to pass that there began to be a great dearth upon the land . . . there was no rain. . . . And there came forth poisonous serpents . . . and did poison many people. And . . . their flocks began to flee before the poisonous serpents, towards the land southward, which was called by the Nephites Zarahemla." (Ether 9:30-31.)[18]

The Lord had two reasons for bringing forth the serpents. One was to call the people to repentance; for they "believed not the words of the prophets, but they cast them out. . . ." (Ether 9:29.) The other was to prepare the land (1 Nephi 2:20) southward with "the cow and the ox, and the ass and the horse" (1 Nephi 18:25) for flocks and herds, and with "all manner of wild animals" (Alma 22:31), for the habitations of the Nephites, the Lamanites, and the Mulekites. The Jaredites of course carried to the new land seeds, animals, birds, fresh-water fish, and many other things needful for food. (Ether 2:1-3.) Apparently Lehi, on the other hand, took very little food other than seed and provisions for their journey. (1 Nephi 18:6.)

Naturally the Jaredite herdsmen kept their flocks and herds under close watch, rounding up any that went astray. But the Lord caused poisonous serpents to drive some of the flocks and herds along the narrow neck of land and into the land southward. After a sufficient number had crossed, "the Lord did cause the serpents that they should pursue them [the flocks] no more, but that they should hedge up the way that the people could not pass [to drive them back], that whoso should attempt to pass might fall by the poisonous serpents." (Ether 9:33.)

Serpents continued to hedge up the way for several hundred years. (Ether 9:31; 10:19.) When the Lord was satisfied that the animals to the south had multiplied sufficiently he removed the "plague of snakes." (Ether 10:19.)

---

[18]Ordinarily the Cordillera Oriental, or east Andes mountains, are rain-soaked, receiving as much as two hundred inches of rain a year. With the absence of the rain, poisonous serpents would have moved up into the cool, high Andes in search of water.

South America has many poisonous snakes. For example, the coral, which averages three feet in length; the cascabel, a four- to five-foot South American rattlesnake of the most dangerous kind (the Indians believe it breaks its victim's neck when it strikes, due to the effect the poison has on the nerves and muscles of the neck); the bushmaster, which measures nine to twelve feet, though it is not so dangerous as the others due to its nocturnal habits; and the fer-de-lance, four to five feet, which has venom to match that of the cobra.

From that time forth the people were able to pass in safety into the land southward to hunt. Following the removal of the serpents the people moved out onto the narrow neck of land and built a great city "by the narrow neck of land" (Ether 10:20), that is, on the shores of the Gulf of Guayaquil.

The Jaredites prospered and multiplied and became "... as numerous as the hosts of Israel." (Mosiah 8:8.) A span of over two thousand years had passed since the Jaredites had left the old country. Now, at this point in their history, they were saturated in sin and ripe for destruction.

Carved stone depicting warrior (Colombia)

CHAPTER 4

Jaredite War Zones

Valley of Gilgal

"Coriantumr was king over all the land," (Ether 12:1) and a man of war. Shared was a man of intrigue, instigator of a power struggle. Their armies "did meet in the valley of Gilgal. . . ." (Ether 13:27.) With nothing more than a name to go by, we are left wondering just where that valley may have been. Cities and lands already tentatively located may help. So perhaps will a clear idea of the location of the ruling city during Coriantumr's reign.

It will be recalled that the land of the Jaredites' first inheritance was Moron (Ether 7:16, 17), presumed to have been near today's Riobamba in the south-central part of the inter-Andean highlands. (See chapter 3, heading "Moron.") Early in Jaredite history Corihor changed the ruling city from Moron to Nehor, which we have suggested was in the foothills west of the Cordillera Occidental, near Manta. Before the Jaredite nation was destroyed, however, the seat of government had switched back to Moron. (See footnote 10 of chapter 3.) We see this from the statement that the brother of Shared "came forth to the land of Moron, and placed himself upon the throne of Coriantumr." (Ether 14:6.)

Since Coriantumr ruled from Moron, it is most likely that he gathered his troops together there. South of Riobamba or Moron is less favorable terrain leading to Desolation and the narrow neck of land, while east and west are mountains. The reasonable assumption, then, is that the valley of Gilgal, where Shared's army met Coriantumr's, was somewhere north of Moron.

A look at the heart of the inter-Andean highlands or plains shows that Quito — often referred to as the Quito basin, the Quito bowl, or the Quito valley — could easily have been the valley of Gilgal. Quito is about 110 miles north of Riobamba, our proposed land of Moron. A few miles north and east of Quito are the fertile Anaquito plains, today a suburb of Quito. This place would have been a convenient spot for a rebel army such as Shared's to form. (See map, "Jaredite War Zones.")

Several passes move out of the Quito basin: one, eastward into the Amazon; another, westward into a tropical rain forest, or wilderness, on the western slopes of the Cordillera Occidental; a third, southward onto the plains near Latacunga, Ambato, and Riobamba; and a fourth, northward to the plains of Anaquito and the gorge of Guaillabamba.

Plains of Heshlon

Coriantumr forced Shared onto the plains of Heshlon. (Ether 13:28.) As stated above, the fertile Anaquito plains are directly north and east of the valley. Just beyond these plains, before the descent into the great gorge of Guaillabamba, are the dry Calderon plains. These plains or the Anaquito plains, or both, may be identified with the plains of Heshlon.

Wilderness of Akish

The fighting moved back from the plains of Heshlon to the valley of Gilgal, where Coriantumr killed Shared. (Ether

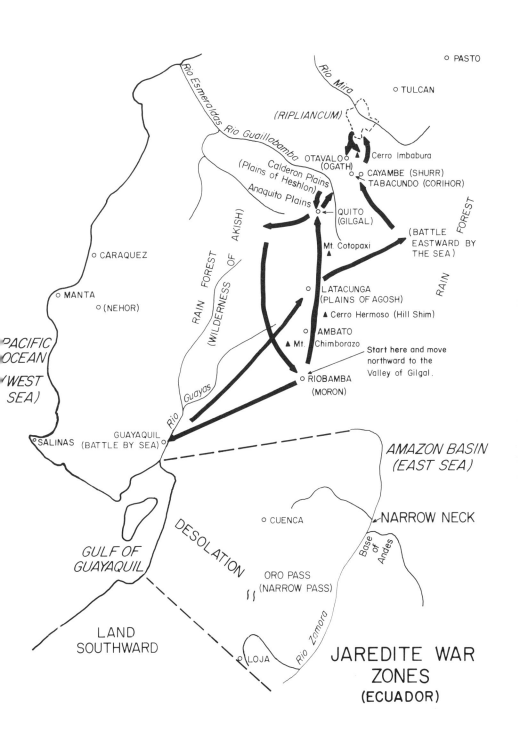

13:29-30.) Subsequently the brother of Shared came against Coriantumr. (Ether 14:3.) Coriantumr drove him into the wilderness of Akish (Ether 14:3), which may be identified with the rain forest or wilderness area west of the inter-Andean highlands. Even today it is known as the northwest rain forest,[1] and is as dense as the Amazon jungle.[2]

Coriantumr surrounded the enemy in the wilderness of Akish in order to force a surrender. (Ether 14:5.) Days in a tropical rain forest can be monotonous. Its high temperatures and humidity have a tendency to make one listless. Apparently it was at such a time, when Coriantumr's men had been drinking, that the army of the brother of Shared killed many of them. The brother of Shared then marched out of the wilderness and "came forth to the land of Moron, and placed himself upon the throne of Coriantumr." (Ether 14:6.)

Borders upon the Seashore

The reign of the brother of Shared did not last, for he was murdered as he sat upon his throne. (Ether 14:9.) A man named Lib became king. "And . . . in the first year of Lib, Coriantumr came up unto the land of Moron, and gave battle unto Lib." (Ether 14:11.) Coriantumr chased Lib to "the borders upon the seashore" (Ether 14:12-13), which could have been Guayaquil. (See map, "Jaredite War Zones.")

At this place the offensive switched and Lib's army drove Coriantumr into the wilderness of Akish. (Ether 14:14.) The Guayas river would have been the most likely route for Coriantumr through this wilderness.

Plains of Agosh

We know that Coriantumr and his army emerged from the wilderness of Akish onto the plains of Agosh. (Ether 14:15.) Unfortunately, nothing more is said of these plains. Most likely they were near today's Latacunga on the central plains or highlands, south of the Quito basin and north of Riobamba.

---

[1] Loren McIntyre, "Ecuador — Low and Lofty Land Astride the Equator," *National Geographic Magazine*, February 1968, p. 267.

[2] Von Hagen, *Ecuador and the Galapagos*, p. 132.

Lib was killed on the plains of Agosh, and his brother Shiz took over the command of the army. (Ether 14:16-17.) Hostilities continued throughout the land: "Shiz pursued after Coriantumr, and he did overthrow many cities, and he did slay both women and children, and he did burn the cities. And there went a fear of Shiz throughout all the land; yea, a cry went forth throughout the land — Who can stand before the army of Shiz? Behold, he sweepeth the earth before him!" (Ether 14:17-18.)

Eastward to the Seashore

Coriantumr and his followers fled "eastward, even to the borders of the seashore." (Ether 14:26.) This flight may well have been over the same terrain through which Pizarro trudged in the year 1541 at the beginning of his search for the "Land of Cinnamon." The trail runs east from the Quito valley to the Amazon rain forest.

The battle lasted three days. (Ether 14:26.) The destruction among the armies of Shiz was so terrible that they fled before the armies of Coriantumr to the land of Corihor. (Ether 14:27.)

Valley of Corihor and Valley of Shurr

We are not told in which direction Shiz retreated to reach the land of Corihor. We can only assume that, since Coriantumr later made his camp near the "hill Ramah-hill Cumorah" in the northern part of the land (Ether 15:8-11; see also the Introduction, heading "Cumorah"), the tide of battle must have flowed in that direction. The valley Corihor must have been along the way to that hill.

Apparently lands en route and the land of Corihor were populated, since Shiz and his army "swept off the inhabitants before them, all them that would not join them." (Ether 14:27.) Because of the terrain of the highlands, many roads, villages, and cities occupy the exact spot today that they did in the days of the ancients. With this thought in mind, our attention is directed to the most likely spot for the valley of Corihor. It is today's Tabacundo, directly north and east of the great gorge of Guaillabamba. Today's modern maps show only two roads leading out of Tabacundo. One moves southwest to the gorge of Guaillabamba, the other runs due east to the village of Cayambe. From whichever direction Coriantumr may have approached this proposed land of Corihor, Shiz would have had an escape route.

Cayambe is about four to eight miles east of Tabacundo and could easily have been the valley of Shurr. This sprawling village rests at the western foot of the beautiful 19,160-foot volcano Cayambe. Three roads lead out of this village. The first road moves to the southwest over bleak highlands, then down toward the gorge of Guaillabamba. The second road runs northward over a divide or ridge into Imbabura. (From this ridge rivers flow north into Imbabura and south to the gorge of Guaillabamba.) The third road moves due west to Tabacundo.

After Coriantumr reached the valley of Shurr he "did gather his armies together upon the hill Comnor, and did sound a trumpet unto the armies of Shiz to invite them forth to battle." (Ether 14:28.) Coriantumr waited upon the slopes of the hill for Shiz to join him. Shiz and his army "came forth" twice (Ether 14:29) and were driven back. The third time so many were killed that the fighting ceased for a time. Coriantumr was carried from the battlefield wounded and Shiz returned to his camp. (Ether 14:30-31.) The hill upon which they fought may have been the volcano Cayambe. Cayambe is called a cerro (hill) by some Ecuadorian map makers. I have in my possession a copy of such a map, a very old map (1490-1533). (See footnote 7, this chapter.)

Waters of Ripliancum

After a period of rest and recuperation, "Shiz did give battle unto the people of Coriantumr." (Ether 15:6.) According to the terrain of the land this attack would have come from both the west (Tabacundo) and the southwest (the gorge of Guaillabamba), leaving Coriantumr with only one escape route — northward. Assuming that our deductions have been correct, he would have found himself in the beautiful land of

Jaredite War Zones 55

Imbabura, Ecuador's lake district. As stated before, Imbabura is a land of many waters and many rivers. (See chapter 3, "Place Where the Nephites Were Destroyed.")

Pressed by his antagonist, Coriantumr continued northward until "he came to the waters of Ripliancum, which, by interpretation, is large, or to exceed all. . . ." (Ether 15:8.) Northward in the land of Imbabura there is a very large, very low, flat area (2,500 feet) surrounded by a high terrace (7,000 and 8,000 feet). At the southern end of this lowland the "waters" of three rivers (the Ambi, the Chorlavi, and the Taguando) meet to flow into the Mira river. The Mira, in turn, cuts through the Cordillera Occidental to flow into the Pacific Ocean. (See map "Hill Ramah-Hill Cumorah.")[3] Could the "waters" of the merging rivers have been called Ripliancum?

When the rains come and the Andean snows melt, the rivers are full.[4] Therefore, it is entirely possible that the merging rivers, Ambi, Chorlavi, and Taguando, which flow into the Mira, formed a river junction which, in the words of the Jaredites, was Ripliancum, "large, or to exceed all." This river junction, coupled with seasonal flooding, could have stopped the northward movement of the Jaredite armies.

The highway which leads from Ecuador into Colombia today passes directly through the lowland area. The conquistadores trudged along that route. North of the lowlands the earth appears to be utter desolation, a no-man's-land. Small cactus-like plants grow, but not much else. The barren land continues to the border town of Tulcán (over 9,000 feet). Tulcán is very cold. From there to Pasto, Colombia (8,400 feet), potatoes and cereals are grown.[5] The Inca road

---

[3]Very little, if any, scientific exploration has been done in this region. Little has been written about it.

[4]The southern part of the central plateau is arid, with very light rainfall. There are no streams except from melting snows. Further north the rainfall is heavier, giving rise to a considerable number of small streams, some of which help to form Ecuador's three great, westward flowing, river systems — the Guayas (which is a part of the Guayaquil estuary), the Esmeraldas (Guaillabamba is its largest tributary), and the Mira.

[5]East of the lowlands are the high Cordillera Oriental, source of the Mira river, entrance into the Amazon basin; west of the lowlands are the Cordillera Occidental, through which the Mira passes.

ends at Pasto. (See map, "Inca Roads," chapter 5; also map, "Jaredite War Zones.")

Coriantumr and his men fought a fierce battle at the waters of Ripliancum, and they "caused them [the armies of Shiz] to flee before them; and they did flee southward, and did pitch their tents in a place which was called Ogath." (Ether 15:10.)

Ogath

Directly south of the lowlands (our proposed waters of Ripliancum) is Otavalo, a small town known for its weavers of wool. Otavalo sits southwest of a great hill called cerro (hill) Imbabura. Otavalo may well have been Ogath.

Hill Ramah-Hill Cumorah

Coriantumr's army followed Shiz as the latter fled. "And . . . [they] did pitch their tents by the hill Ramah; and it was that same hill where my father Mormon did hide up the records unto the Lord, which were sacred." (Ether 15:11.) If the cerro (hill) Imbabura was the hill Ramah-hill Cumorah, Coriantumr presumably camped at the northern foot of the hill while Shiz camped a short distance from its southwestern foot.

According to a Jewish scholar I consulted, who had recently returned from Jerusalem, *Ramah* means height, high place, or plateau. He gave as an example the Golan Heights, which in Hebrew is "Ramat ha Golan," *Ramat* meaning "heights of." This meaning is confirmed by the *Dictionary of the Bible,* which states that Ramah is "the name of several places in Palestine, so called from their 'loftiness,' that being the radical meaning of the word. . . ."[6] Accordingly if the Jaredites named their hill, as they named the waters of Ripliancum, for certain characteristics, the name "the hill Ramah" could signify a hill which rises up from a highland or plateau, or a hill of imposing height. Either description alone, or both together, fit perfectly the cerro Imbabura,

---

[6]James Hastings (ed.), *Dictionary of the Bible* (New York: Charles Scribner's Sons, 1952), p. 782.

which rises up from the elevated inter-Andean highlands. Most cerros in Ecuador differ from the cerro Imbabura in that they rise up from the Cordilleras themselves rather than from the high plateau.

The cerro (hill) Imbabura (15,033 feet)[7] stands about 7,000 feet above the highlands. It can be seen for miles around. It is midway between the two great ranges (the Cordillera Oriental and the Cordillera Occidental) and belongs to a mountain knot which unites them.

The cerro Imbabura is an extinct volcano which, when active, has bubbled up mud and water. Since the time of the ancients it has been worshipped as a God.[8] Even today the natives come to the hill to ask for a favor. Native Imbaburians say the hill is no longer lit. For this reason an Indian will light a cigarette and blow the smoke toward the hill. Only then will he ask his favor. He always begins his request by saying, "Daddy Imbabura."

Since the hill is considered sacred, the names given to certain sections of it may represent events which have taken place on its slopes. I note that, on a detailed map of the cerro Imbabura which I have in my possession, such names as Batallón (Battalion) Imbabura, Compania (Company) Imbabura, and Zapallo Loma (in Ecuadorian, *sad person hill*), are given to parts of the hill. It is a very interesting hill indeed.

Coriantumr's Wanderings

A truce prevailed throughout the land for four years. Coriantumr and Shiz spent that time gathering to their armies every man, woman, and child from all parts of the land. Each man decided which of the two armies he would fight in, and his family enlisted with him, women and children being armed like the men. While the book of Ether does not say so specifically, it would appear that the gathering places for the

---

[7] It is presumed that the volcanos (often called cerros or hills) of Ecuador and Peru are the hills of the Book of Mormon. To many, cerro Imbabura, Cayambe, and Hermoso would be mountains, but one man's mountain can be another man's hill.

[8] Peter Schmid, *Beggars on Golden Stools,* translated by Mervyn Savill (New York: Frederick Praeger, Inc., 1956), p. 173.

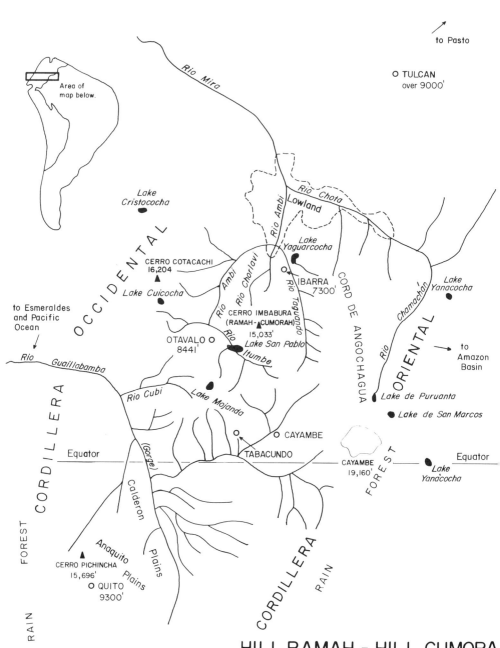

HILL RAMAH - HILL CUMORA
(NORTHERN ECUADOR)

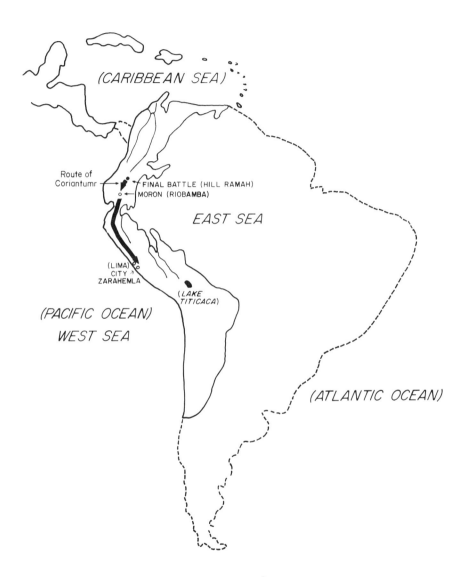

CORIANTUMR'S WANDERINGS

two armies were the respective campsites indicated earlier — Ogath and the hill Ramah.

With the great gathering accomplished, the annihilating war was resumed; and it continued until only Shiz and Coriantumr remained alive. When Shiz fainted from the loss of blood the weary Coriantumr leaned upon his sword to rest. After a short while he cut off the head of Shiz.

Coriantumr soon would have found that he was the last survivor.[9] Presumably he made his way southward through the gorge of Guaillabamba and on until he came to the land of Moron. Perhaps he hoped that somehow some of his people had escaped annihilation.

It is not clear how Coriantumr got into Mulekite territory, the land of Zarahemla in the land southward. Since the Mulekites had lived there since their landing (Omni 16), either they must have found Coriantumr while exploring the land northward and taken him back with them, or he must have found his way to the land of Zarahemla. No time span is given for his solitary journeyings. The record merely says that he "was discovered by the people of Zarahemla; and he dwelt with them for the space of nine moons." (Omni 21.)

Hundreds of years later, after the Nephite-Mulekite merger, "there was a large stone brought unto [Mosiah] with engravings on it; and he did interpret the engravings. . . . And they gave an account of one Coriantumr, and the slain of his people. . . ." (Omni 20-21.) The logical conclusion is that the engraver was Coriantumr. Perhaps he wrote on the stone in Zarahemla. What better would the sole survivor of a great nation do, especially when language differences precluded him from properly communicating his story to his hosts? But the stone was evidently portable, so he may have written it before being discovered by the people of Zarahemla.

Whatever the unknown details, the results fulfilled the Lord's word that Coriantumr would live only to see another people inherit the land and that they would bury him. (Ether 13:21.)

---

[9]The prophet Ether also remained. Ether had hidden in a cave until the fighting was over. (Ether 13:13-14, 18, 22; 15:33.)

Part III
The Land Southward

Llama (high inter-Andean plains)

CHAPTER 5
Lands Nephi-Lehi

Nephite Landing

As we have seen, "the land southward" was all the land occupied by the Nephites and Lamanites south of the narrow neck of land. Since the movement of the Nephites away from the Lamanites was always generally in a northerly direction, we would expect the place of Lehi's landing to be well in the southern portion of the land southward. The Book of Mormon gives no clue as to that landing place, saying merely, "after we had sailed for the space of many days we did arrive at the promised land. . . ." (1 Nephi 18:23.)

A more specific statement on this has come to us from the early days of the Church, and for a long time was generally accepted as a revelation to Joseph Smith. While the statement cannot be definitely substantiated as a revelation, it is acknowledged to be in the handwriting of Frederick G. Williams, counselor to Joseph Smith in the First Presidency, and is written on the same loose sheet of paper as an undoubted revelation in the same hand. Especially in view of the categorical nature of the statement, it would be difficult to believe that it did not emanate from, or at least have the approval of, the Prophet Joseph himself. It says that Lehi's group sailed from Arabia, "in a southeast direction, and landed on the continent of South America, in Chili, thirty degrees south latitude."[1] Orson Pratt more than once referred to this landing "on the coast of Chile,"[2] and there are other nineteenth-century references in similar terms. The 30° latitude would put the landing near today's Coquimbo, Chile, about 220 miles north of Santiago.

Following the landing, all efforts were turned toward settling that quarter of the land. Tents were pitched, seeds were planted, and scouts were sent into the forests, where beasts of every kind were found. (1 Nephi 18:25.) Several hundred years prior to the Nephite landing, flocks and herds from the Jaredite civilization had migrated from the land northward (Ether 9:31-32; 10:19) to as far south as the forests of Chile. As mentioned previously, through this migration the Lord was preparing the land southward as a habitation for the immigrants from Jerusalem. (1 Nephi 2:20.)

Besides beasts in the forests in the new land, Lehi's group discovered "all manner of ore, both of gold, and of silver, and of copper." (1 Nephi 18:25.) Large ore deposits are still to be found in South America; as a matter of fact, Chile has the biggest "open-pit" copper mine in the world.

Apparently Nephi lived only a short time near the place of the landing, just long enough to do some planting, harvesting, and exploring before he had to flee into the wilderness. (2 Nephi 5:5.) The Lamanites remained in Chile, but they were an idle people lacking permanent homes, "dwelling in tents, and wandering about in the wilderness with a short skin girdle about their loins and their heads shaven. . . ." (Enos 20.) This would explain why scientific expeditions have not found ruins in Chile to match those further north in Peru, Central America, and Mexico.

---

[1]As quoted in U.A.S. Newsletter (Provo, Utah: University Archaeological Society at Brigham Young University), January 30, 1963, p. 7.

[2]Orson Pratt, *Journal of Discourses* (London, England: Albert Carrington, 1869), vol. 12, p. 342.

Nephi

Nephi, his wife, and his little band of followers journeyed "many days" before they pitched their tents. (2 Nephi 5:7.) The Book of Mormon does not specify the course of their journey, but a clue may be obtained from the "rememberers" of history and mythology. The "rememberers" tell of a man called Manco Capac, his three brothers, and their *sister-wives;* a little band of wandering people who came to Cuzco from the direction of Lake Titicaca. Manco Capac carried a golden staff in his hand which had been given to him by the Sun God. This staff was to show him the place the Sun God wished him to settle; for it would sink into the ground at that place with one blow.

Manco Capac, it is said, moved northward from Titicaca through the fourteen-thousand-foot LaRaya pass (which separates the Titicaca basin from the Vilcañota valley) and on to Cuzco. Near Cuzco he drove his golden staff into the ground; it quickly disappeared. The sign had been given, and he knew that his wanderings were over.[3]

Legends are often modified historical accounts. The title Manco Capac means "royal master" or "chief," a reasonable approximation to the title by which Nephi's people knew him. (2 Nephi 5:8, 9, 18; Jacob 1:9-11.) There is a parallel too between Manco Capac's golden staff and the brass ball of curious workmanship which Nephi carried with him into the wilderness. "And I, Nephi . . . brought . . . the ball, or compass, which was prepared for my father by the hand of the Lord. . . ." (2 Nephi 5:12. See also 1 Nephi 16:10, 16, 26-30.) Nephi's brass ball, or director, served the same purpose as Manco Capac's golden staff. The possessor of each was shown the land in which he should settle. Both the brass ball and the golden staff were given to man by God.

Manco Capac, it is said, was pale-faced or white.[4] Garcilaso de la Vega, a Spanish chronicler, whose father was

---

[3]Garcilaso de la Vega, *The Incas,* 1539-1616, translated by Maria Jolas (New York: Grossman Publishers, 1961), p. 5.

[4]Bertrand Flornoy, *World of the Incas* (New York: Vanguard Press, 1965), p. 118.

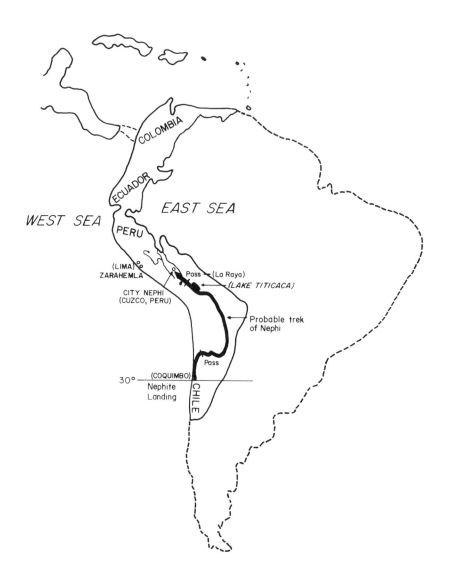

a conquistadore and his mother an Inca, wrote that Manco Capac and his *sister-wife,* between them, taught the people the arts and industries; he instructed the men in agriculture and introduced the laws of society, she taught the women to spin and weave.[5] Nephi wrote, "And I did teach my people to build buildings, and to work in all manner of wood, and of iron, and of copper, and of brass, and of steel, and of gold, and of silver, and of precious ores, which were in great abundance. . . . And . . . I . . . did cause my people to be industrious, and to labor with their hands." (2 Nephi 5:15, 17.)

Those familiar with the Manco Capac story usually interpret the term *sister-wife* to mean that he married his blood-sister. To one who knows the Book of Mormon story of Lehi's and Ishmael's families, however, the real meaning of *sister-wife* becomes immediately clear. "And . . . I, Nephi, took one of the [five] daughters of Ishmael to wife; and also, my brethren [Laman, Lemuel, Sam] took of the daughters of Ishmael to wife. . . ." (1 Nephi 16:7.) Would not these women logically be called sister-wives?

From the striking similarities between the two accounts it seems clear that the legend of Manco Capac is a reflection of the story of Nephi, his wife, and his little band of followers in their flight from Chile to Cuzco, Peru, somewhere around 585 B.C. as recorded in 2 Nephi 5:5-7.[6]

Inca Roads

The Inca roads span a distance of over two thousand miles, from the northern borders of Ecuador to central Chile. They were my chief guide to the widely separated lands and cities of the Nephites.

---

[5]Garcilaso, *The Incas,* pp. 11-12.
[6]Some historians date Manco Capac *after* the time of Christ, thus attributing the building of the great stone cities to that time. However, A. Hyatt Verrill reports that it would have been impossible to accomplish such feats of construction and engineering found in the area of Cuzco during the relatively short period of time allotted between Manco Capac and Atahualpa Inca (about A.D. 930 to A.D. 1530). (Verrill and Verrill, *America's Ancient Civilizations,* p. 213.)
Philip Ainsworth Means states, "The origin of the great [Inca] dynasty . . . is still . . . shrouded in mystery." (Means, *Ancient Civilizations of the Andes,* p. 205.)

There were two major highways. The first and most important highway ran north-south from a point north of Quito, Ecuador, through to Cuzco, Peru, and on to Mendoza, Argentina. From Mendoza the highway turned westward to Santiago, Chile, on the Pacific coast, and then southward to Talca. Along this route the road moved through rugged mountains which were often so high that the bottom was not visible. In some sections the road moved through tunnels cut out of solid rock, and steps were formed to ascend or descend great heights. In other sections the road spanned immense swamp-lands.

The second highway ran the full length of the coast of Peru. It started at Tumbes near southern Ecuador and moved south to Arequipa, Peru, and possibly further, into Chile. This road often moved over deserts of intense heat. Periodically, lateral roads connected it to the high Andean highway described in the previous paragraph.

Along the Inca road, at distances equal to a day's journey, were stone tambos, or way-stations, serving as resting houses for weary travelers. Usually a storehouse was located near the tambo. If not, frequently the tambo itself would be stocked with "freeze-dried"[7] potatoes (usually of the purple variety), meat, and dried corn or maize.

It seems likely that the first section of this famous road system was constructed in the vicinity of Cuzco and Titicaca during the time of Nephi, which was about 588-544 B.C. (See next section, "City of Nephi," where that city is identified with Cuzco.) The average width of the road in this section was about fifteen feet.[8]

---

[7]Freeze-dried foods were common to the Inca. They carried meat, fish, and potatoes up into the high Andes to expose them to bitter cold nights. The food would freeze, then partially thaw the next day, then freeze again the next night. This process removed the moisture, leaving a dry, nearly imperishable material. To bring it back to life they boiled it in water.

[8]The description of the magnificent Inca road sounds very much like the famous ancient Incense road at Sheba in today's Yemen. Lehi may have traveled on or near sections of this famous road after moving inland from the Red Sea.

Like the Incense roads, portions of the Inca roads were paved with flat stones while other sections were merely stretches of hard-packed earth. Low stone walls on either side of the road marked the way of the Incense road, likewise the Inca road. Steep inclines on the Inca road were approached like those at Sheba,

INCA ROADS

Other sections of the road apparently were constructed at a date much later than the first one, a fact which fits with the move of the Nephite people away from the city and land of Nephi and into other parts of the island. These roads were wider than the first; they averaged about twenty-four feet. It seems probable that this magnificent road system was not completely bound together until about the year A.D. 29 or 30 when "many highways [were] cast up, and many roads made, which led from city to city, and from land to land, and from place to place." (3 Nephi 6:8.)

Victor von Hagen, the famous Inca road explorer, had an abounding respect for the men who built this famous road. He said: "O! what greater things could have been said of Alexander the Great or any of the powerful kings who have ruled the world than that they could have made such a road as this . . . the grandest . . . road in the world."[9]

City of Nephi

The city of Cuzco is situated in an Andean valley, 11,207 feet above sea level. Anciently it was known as the "Navel of the Universe" and the "Center of the Inca world."[10] Garcilaso tells us that the city was divided into two distinct districts, Hurin-Cuzco (Lower-Cuzco) and Hanan-Cuzco (Upper-Cuzco). Hurin-Cuzco was the more ancient of the two. I believe Hurin-Cuzco to be the site of the city of Nephi which at a later date, under Lamanite influence, was referred to as the city of Lehi-Nephi. (2 Nephi 5:15-17; Mosiah 9:8.)

The ancient city of Cuzco (including both Hurin and Hanan) was laid out in large blocks or squares with straight, paved streets. It had large plazas, public baths, a house of

---

with gradual steps. The same method of cutting through solid rock, when necessary, was also used.

The engineering method of the whole road was like that of the Sabaeans or the people of Saba (the biblical Sheba). I believe that if the experts were to study the engineering methods of these roads, Incense and Inca, they would find them to be amazingly similar. (Wendell Phillips, *Qataban and Sheba*, Collins-Knowlton-Wing, Inc., 1955. Von Hagen, *Highway of the Sun*.

[9]Von Hagen, *Highway of the Sun*, p. 305.

[10]If the Inca Empire were to be thought of as a tall, thin man stretching from Ecuador and the narrow neck of land southward into Chile, Cuzco would be located at about the place where the navel would be.

learning, and factories where the women spun and wove cloth of great beauty. Hurin-Cuzco had a Sun Temple. This we would expect, since Nephi built "a temple . . . after the manner of the temple of Solomon." (2 Nephi 5:16.) An interview with Rabbi Maurice Jaffee, as reported in the *Oakland Tribune* (June 21, 1974) by George W. Cornell, revealed that Solomon's temple was built of a special radiant stone called Jerusalem's "golden stone," whose color changed from gray to white to gold, depending on the angle in which the sun struck it.

In Hurin-Cuzco today the church of Santo Domingo sits atop the perfectly cut stone foundation of the ancient Sun Temple which undoubtedly was once the Nephites' "House of the Lord." Spanish chronicles report that at one time this temple was adorned on the outside with gold plate, beaten as thin as onion-skin paper. Hernando de Soto first saw Cuzco at sunset and ". . . as the retreating sun's rays touched the beaten gold plates that adorned its walls, the pyramided Sun Temple, towering over the lower buildings around it, gleamed as if it were cast in metal."[11]

During the reign of king Noah a great deal of fine work was done "within the walls of the temple. . . ." (Mosiah 11:10.) This included fine wood ornamented with gold and silver and copper and brass. Garcilaso, in his description of Cuzco's Sun Temple, told of the beautiful temple garden which was entirely made of gold and silver. There were plants of all kinds, animals, and crawling things such as the snake and lizard, all made of these precious metals.[12] Garcilaso did not mention items made of copper and brass, but that does not necessarily mean that there were none.

Inside the main room of the Sun Temple, behind the altar, hung a huge golden plaque with the likeness of the sun, a round face with prolonged rays or flames. On either side of the sun disc were golden thrones, or seats, elevated on plaques of the same metal. The seats faced the audience. Historians say that they were used as thrones upon which

---
[11]Von Hagen, *Highway of the Sun,* pp. 81, 88.
[12]Garcilaso, *The Incas,* p. 80.

mummy bundles of past kings were seated.[13] The book of Mosiah suggests another use for these seats. "And the seats which were set apart for the high priests, which were above all the other seats, he [king Noah] did ornament with pure gold. . . ." (Mosiah 11:11.)

North of the temple, adjoining a public square, was a tower. Garcilaso said: "The walls were about twelve feet in height, but the roof was so high that the whole thing stood above all the towers I have ever seen in Spain, except the one in Seville."[11] He also said that on top of the roof there "was a tall, sturdy spire" which added greatly to its height. The inside height, from the ground to the top of the roof, was over sixty feet.[15] This structure was torn down while Garcilaso still lived. Could this have been the "tower near the temple; yea, a very high tower, even so high that he [king Noah] could stand upon the top thereof and overlook the land. . ."? (Mosiah 11:12.)

Nephi said, "And I did teach my people to build buildings. . . ." (2 Nephi 5:15.) He must have brought such knowledge with him from the Old World.[16] Still standing in Cuzco are buildings of dressed (cut) stone, the stones fitted together without mortar so perfectly that the thin blade of a knife cannot be inserted between them. It was a work almost

---

[13]There were twelve kings mentioned in Spanish chronicles, including Inca Huascar. Inca Huascar and his half-brother Atahualpa, governor of Quito, were both alive when Pizarro entered Peru.

[14]Garcilaso, *The Incas,* p. 353.

[15]Garcilaso, *The Incas,* p. 353.

[16]Cuzco's stone buildings are like that of Sheba's (near the Red Sea) in that they were built of cut stone put together without mortar. Wendell Phillips, a famous American scholar, said that he saw an irrigation system and parts of the famous giant dam at Sheba in Yemen. He said sections of the dam were still standing. They were built of huge boulders perfectly cut and put together. "We saw no trace of mortar of any kind, yet we looked at portions of the wall that were more than fifty feet high, standing as they had when Sheba's great artisans built them. . . ." (Wendell Phillips, *Qataban and Sheba,* p. 222.)

Sand removed from other buildings such as the temple at Sheba revealed beautifully cut limestone blocks put together without mortar. (Thomas J. Abercrombie, "Behind the Veil of Troubled Yemen," *National Geographic Magazine,* March 1964, p. 409.)

The art of stonecutting has made Cuzco famous. It stands as strong presumptive evidence that Nephi, after sojourning for years as a stranger in a strange land (1 Nephi 17:4), carried this knowledge to America.

indestructible. Two streams, the Rodadero and the Huatanay, paralleled each other through Cuzco at a distance of about fifteen hundred feet, providing the city with water. Hurin-Cuzco, with its temple, stone buildings, paved roads, and irrigation, must indeed have been to Nephi his "City Beautiful."

The Land (County) Nephi

Within the boundaries of the county land of Nephi were the cities of Nephi (later, under Lamanite influence, called Lehi-Nephi) and Shilom (Mosiah 9:8), with their surrounding agricultural lands. The land Shemlon (Mosiah 11:12) and Mormon (Alma 5:3) are also mentioned. Doubtless there were others.

The original county land of Nephi was bounded by the Cordillera Vilcabamba on the north, and by the Cordillera Carabaya on the east (with the Vilcañota mountains running within the borders parallel to the Carabaya). The southern border was formed by a mountain knot, or knudo, called the Vilcañota knudo. Manco Capac (Nephi) moved over this mountain knot, which now separates the department of Cuzco from the Titicaca basin, via the LaRaya pass. The western boundary would have been the gorge of the deep Apurimac river, a tributary of today's Amazon. (See map, "Original Boundaries of the County Land of Nephi.") The Apurimac river was, and still is, in many places, about 250 feet wide and, at certain times of the year, over eighty feet deep. The word *apurimac* means "Great Speaker."[17] The river gets its Indian or Quechua name from the fact that one can hear the dread river's dull roar for miles around. When one is standing close to the river it is often impossible to shout above the deafening roar, and sign language must be used to communicate. The difficulties of crossing such a great river would have made the Apurimac a natural barrier and the most likely western border for the land Nephi.

The city of Cuzco sat near the northern border of the land, at the northern end of the valley. (See map, "Original Boundaries of the County Land of Nephi.") Cuzco's front

---

[17]Hiram Bingham, *Lost City of the Incas* (Hawthorn Books, Inc., 1948), p. 99.

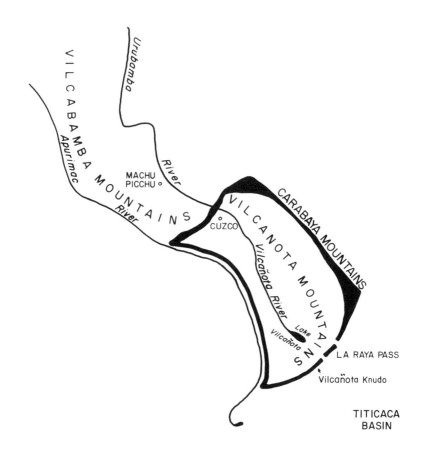

ORIGINAL BOUNDARIES OF
THE COUNTY LAND OF NEPHI

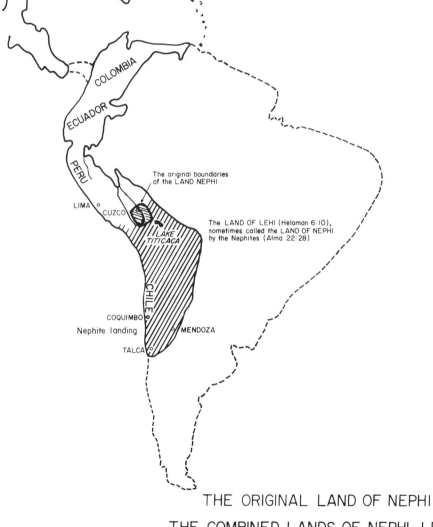

side (Hurin-Cuzco) faced south while "the back side of the city" (Mosiah 22:6) (Hanan-Cuzco) pushed up against the Sacsahuaman hill on its north.

At the time of the conquistadores, Cuzco had four principal highways which led to all parts of the land. (See map, "Inca Roads.") One road, the Cuntusuyu road, led out of Cuzco in a southwesterly direction to a place south of Nazca. It will be discovered later in this book that all the land south of Nazca was Lamanite territory. (See map "Battle by West Sea"; also, Alma 22:28.) Assuming that Hurin-Cuzco was the city of Nephi, this road would not have been built until after the city of Nephi had come under Lamanite control.

Another road, the Collasuyu road, moved southward to the LaRaya pass and the Titicaca basin. The Collasuyu road presumably would have been fully developed early in Nephite history. (See section headed, "Wind-Furnaces.")

The next road, the Antisuyu road, stretched eastward towards Pisac, then northward into the Urubamba river valley. This road too could have been fully developed early in Nephite history.

The last road, the Chinchasuyu road, moved in a northwesterly direction. It crossed over the Apurimac river by way of a great suspension bridge, known in literature as the "Bridge of San Luis Rey." The Chinchasuyu road was a part of the great Inca highland road which stretched from Pasto, Colombia, through Cuzco, and on to Talca, Chile. It was upon this road that the conquistadores entered Cuzco. The county land of Zarahemla would have begun a few miles north of the suspension bridge. (See map, "Zarahemla and the Sidon river.")

Obviously there were no roads leading to Zarahemla when Mosiah and his people were led there from the land of Nephi (Omni 13); nor were there roads for Limhi and his people to follow to the city Zarahemla. (Mosiah 7:4; 8:7-8; 22:11.) As long as the Nephites and Lamanites were at war there would have been no roads constructed connecting the county land of Nephi and the county land of Zarahemla.

It seems safe to say, then, that if Hurin-Cuzco were the city Nephi, the Chinchasuyu road would not have been built until late in Nephite history (Helaman 6:7-8), perhaps as late as the time of Christ when "there were many highways cast up, and many roads made, which led from city to city, and from land to land, and from place to place." (3 Nephi 6:8.) On this basis, from the days of Nephi down to king Limhi (about 120 B.C.), the main exit from the land of Nephi would have been through what is called today the LaRaya pass and into the Titicaca basin.

Wind-Furnaces

"And I, Nephi, did take the sword of Laban, and after the manner of it did make many swords, lest by any means the people who were now called Lamanites should come upon us and destroy us. . . ." (2 Nephi 5:14.)

To make swords of steel, Nephi would have needed a smelter or wind-furnace. Outside the proposed southeastern borders of the land of Nephi (southward over the LaRaya pass and eastward into the Carabaya) archaeologists have found on the tops of the highest hills this very thing; wind-furnaces which were "circular in shape with the tunnel or mouth . . . facing the windward side, so that the strong winds [from the Amazon] produced sufficient draft to obtain the high temperatures . . . necessary to melt the gold. . . ,"[18] or, presumably, any other ore which may have been used. The engineering idea of "forced-air draft" is a principle for refining ore that Nephi must have carried with him to the New World. It was the governing principle of Solomon's smelter which stood at the tip of the Gulf of Aqabah to catch the strong winds which blew up from the Wadi Arabah.[19] Lehi must

---

[18] Von Hagen, *Highway of the Sun,* p. 77.

[19] Solomon's smelter was situated halfway between the east and west sides of the Arabah rift. The principles governing this smelter were unique in that it required no hand bellows to fan the flames in the furnace rooms, but depended on strong winds that blew constantly up from the Wadi Arabah.

Negev archaeologist Dr. Nelson Glueck commented on the fact that Solomon's engineers used the Bessemer principle of forced-air draft, discovered in modern times a little more than a century ago. (Nelson Glueck, *Rivers in the Desert,* Farrar, Straus and Giroux, Inc., 1959, pp. 164-165.)

have lived near Solomon's smelter for a time. His first camp was by what Nephi called "the fountain [or headwater] of the Red Sea." (1 Nephi 2:9.) This would presumably have been the Gulf of Aqabah.

Fortifying Nephite Cities

The Lamanites found the valley to which Nephi had fled and, as Nephi had feared, wars commenced between the two groups of people. Eventually the disputes became so severe that the Nephites were forced to ". . . fortify [their] cities, or whatsoever place of [their] inheritance." (Jarom 7.) The cities near the southern borders would have been the most vulnerable, because the Lamanites would have entered the valley through the LaRaya pass. Hurin-Cuzco (Nephi), on the other hand, would have been the least vulnerable because of its northerly position.

Though the Nephites were busy fortifying their cities they still found time to develop the land's mineral resources, for they "became exceeding rich in gold, and in silver and in precious things. . . ." (Jarom 8.) Even down to the time of Pizarro, large gold nuggets were panned (not mined) from a river, called by the Spanish conquerors "the verie riche river of Carabaya." These nuggets were washed down from the hills during the flooding season and were collected when the water was low.[20]

Archaeologists have found in the Carabaya country, miners' homes built of stone and other evidences of mining operations, indicating that perhaps this area was fully developed at the time the fortifications arose around the cities in the land Nephi. The Book of Mormon record for around 400 B.C. says that the Nephites "multiplied exceedingly, and spread upon the face of the land." (Jarom 8.)

Nephites Go to Zarahemla

Perhaps 350 years after Lehi left Jerusalem the Lord warned Mosiah (probably because of the frequency and severity of the Lamanite attacks) to "flee out of the land of Nephi,

---

[20]Von Hagen, *Highway of the Sun*, pp. 57, 76, 77.

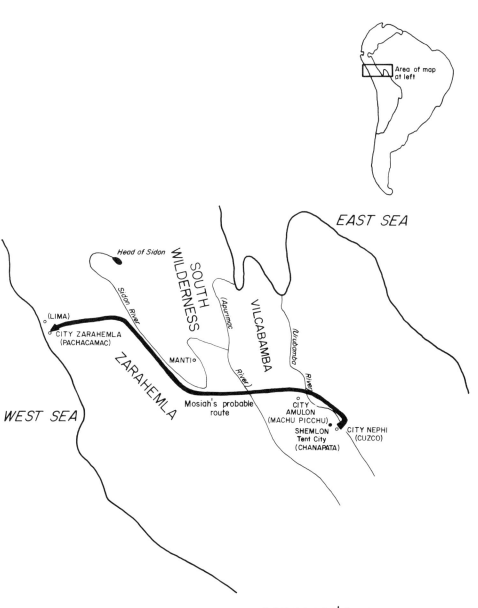

and as many as would hearken unto the voice of the Lord should also depart out of the land with him. . . ." (Omni 12.) The wording suggests a long journey: "They were led by many preachings and prophesyings. And they were admonished continually by the word of God; and they were led by the power of his arm. . . ." Thus they traveled through the mountain wilderness "until they came down [i.e., out of the Andes] into the land which is called the land of Zarahemla." (Omni 13.)[21] This appears to have been about twenty miles south of Lima, Peru. The ruins are called Pachacamac. (See chapter 7.)

The drastic change from the pleasant mountain valleys to the coastal deserts must have been stifling to the Nephites. Many of them did not want to stay in Zarahemla. They, or their near descendants, desired to go back "up into the wilderness to return to the land of Nephi . . ." (Omni 27), to their stone houses, rich fields, planted terraces, running water, paved streets and roads, and particularly to their more pleasing climate. In contrast, the desert land of Pachacamac (Zarahemla) rarely has rain. This is because of the cold Humboldt current which moves northward along the Peruvian coast. (See footnote 14, chapter 3.) The coastal homes were usually made of adobe or reeds. So a man named Zeniff led a group of Nephite people back to the mountain land of their forefathers.

Zeniff's Group

When the people of Zeniff arrived at the land of Nephi they found that the Lamanites had moved into the stone city of Nephi. With a few men, Zeniff went into the city to talk to the king, who made an agreement that the Nephite group should possess the land and city of Nephi (which was now

---

[21]Zarahemla was already occupied by a group of people which called themselves Mulekites. They were descendants of Mulek, son of Zedekiah king of Judah, and others who escaped with him from Jerusalem before its destruction. (Omni 15-16; Helaman 6:10.)

The name Mulek may not have been the true name of Zedekiah's son. The Hebrew word MLK, pronounced Mulek, means *king*. Because his father was blinded and in captivity and all his brothers were killed, it may be that this sole surviving son took upon himself the title which was his by inheritance, that of Mulek (king).

called Lehi-Nephi — see footnote 23) and the land and city of Shilom. The Lamanite king permitted this because the Lamanites "were a lazy and an idolatrous people; therefore they were desirous to bring us [the Nephite group] into bondage, that they might glut themselves with the labors of our hands. . . ." (Mosiah 9:12.)

Lamanite Land of Shemlon

After the agreement had been made, the Lamanite king commanded his own people to leave the lands of Nephi and Shilom, and they probably went to the nearby land of Shemlon. (Mosiah 9:7; 10:7.) This land must have been but a few miles from the city of Nephi. We are told that it was possible to overlook the Lamanite land of Shemlon and the Nephite land of Shilom from the top of a tall tower which stood near the temple in the city of Nephi. (Mosiah 11:12.)

Just outside the northwest boundary of Cuzco is an ancient site which archaeologists call Chanapata. This is said to be the oldest site ever discovered in the Cuzco valley. This estimate of its relative antiquity is based on the fact that there are no stone buildings, only evidences of fieldstone walls, simple graves, and general rubble.[22] Such evidence, however, does not necessarily mean that the site is older; it could instead mean that a less civilized people lived there. Thus Chanapata could easily have been the ancient habitation of the Lamanite people who lived near the city of Nephi in the land of Shemlon.

Nephite Land of Shilom

When Zeniff's group entered the city of Nephi they "began to build buildings, and to repair the walls of the city, yea, even the walls of the city of Lehi-Nephi,[23] and the city of Shilom." (Mosiah 9:8.) As stated previously, Cuzco was divided into two distinct districts, Hurin (Lower) Cuzco and

---

[22] T. R. Ybarra, *Lands of the Andes* (New York: Coward-McCann, 1947), pp. 156-157.

[23] Apparently the Lamanites had attached the name Lehi to the city of Nephi, making it the city Lehi-Nephi. This would have indicated their victory over the city. The land south from which the Lamanites came was known as the land of Lehi. (Helaman 6:10.)

Hanan (Upper) Cuzco. Hurin-Cuzco (Lehi-Nephi — see section headed, "City of Nephi") was southeast of the Antisuyu road. The Antisuyu road ran eastward from the main square and divided Hurin-Cuzco from Hanan-Cuzco. Hanan-Cuzco was to the northwest of the Antisuyu road.

It is possible that Hanan-Cuzco was Shilom. Such a close proximity seems implied in the account of when Ammon with fifteen other men came up from Zarahemla to look into the welfare of the people who lived in the city of Nephi. "And when they had wandered forty days they came to a hill, which is north of the land of Shilom, and there they pitched their tents. And Ammon took three of his brethren . . . and they went down into the land of Nephi. And behold, they met the king of the people who were in the land of Nephi, and in the land of Shilom. . . ." (Mosiah 7:5-7.) Although Ammon and his men camped on the hill north of Shilom, the record does not say that they went down into the land (city) of Shilom, but rather that they went down into the land (city) of Nephi. The wording suggests that the land of Lehi-Nephi, as well as the land of Shilom, stood directly below the hill which was north of Shilom. The fact that king Limhi was very cautious about leaving the city Nephi (Mosiah 21:19) similarly suggests that he had not gone far from the city when he met Ammon.

North of Hanan-Cuzco (Shilom) is a hill called Sacsahuaman. On this hill stands a great fortress or citadel. "And he [king Noah] caused a great tower to be built on the hill north of the land Shilom. . . ." (Mosiah 11:13.) Notice that the tower was a *great* tower and not a *tall* tower, indicating that it probably was more than a mere platform from which the countryside could be viewed.

There are several possible definitions of a tower. A tower may be a building which stands above all other buildings, as did the tall tower near the temple in Nephi; or it may be a citadel or fortress; or it may be a structure relatively high by its position. Indeed, the "great tower" spoken of in Mosiah 11:13 could easily have been the "great fortress" of Sacsahuaman.

The Sacsahuaman fortress was built of dressed (cut) stones put together without mortar. It is said that some of the stones used at Sacsahuaman weighed as much as two hundred tons each.[24] Garcilaso describes the northern side of the fortress as having three separate walls, each within the other, with a gate in each wall. These gates were operated like drawbridges by lowering or lifting a huge stone into place. Connected with this fortress was a network of underground passages which ran in every direction. Legends have it that one such passage led from the fortress to the Temple of the Sun in Hurin-Cuzco.[25] Garcilaso said that as a boy he had gone many times to the fortress with his friends, but they had been afraid to venture into the passageways for fear of getting lost.[26] Eventually the Spaniards completely destroyed this network. The existence of the wall and the passageway of the fortress is consistent with the Book of Mormon statement that Gideon was willing to lead the people of king Limhi through "the back wall, on the back side of the city . . . through the secret pass . . . around the land of Shilom." (Mosiah 22:6-8.)

At the time that king Mosiah and his people fled the land of Nephi (Omni 12-13) the hill north of the land Shilom was a "resort" (Mosiah 11:13.) To the Nephites a resort was a small fort. (Alma 48:8.) It would appear therefore that the Sacsahuaman fortress was started in or before the days of Mosiah and was strengthened and enlarged in the days of king Noah. To the archaeologist, the date of the building of the fortress has remained a mystery. Some say it was pre-Inca, others say Inca.

The Hebrew word *shilom* means peace. Peace means a state of tranquillity or quiet. Fields and pastures give one a feeling of peace and tranquillity. Perhaps Shilom and the hill north of it were comprised mostly of fields and pastures, with a few homes scattered throughout. Garcilaso said that the first homes were built on the slopes of the Sacsahuaman hill.

---

[24] Bingham, *Lost City of the Incas,* p. 93.
[25] T. R. Ybarra, *Lands of the Andes,* p. 136.
[26] Garcilaso, *The Incas,* pp. 235-237.

This district in northern Cuzco was called Collcampata. East of Collcampata was a place called Cantutpata, or "district of the very lovely flower." (Cantut is similar to the carnation.) Next was the Pumacurcu district. *Puma* means lion and *curcu* means beam. Here, Garcilaso said, were a number of heavy beams to which lions were tied while they were being tamed for the king.

King Noah built "many buildings . . . in the land Shilom." (Mosiah 11:13.) North of the Antisuyu road and the main square stood a palace called Cora-Cora, or Pastures Palace. It was called this because it was located in some open fields. Behind or north of the Cora-Cora was the teacher's house (Yachahuasi) or school. Beside or west of the Cora-Cora was a large building called Cassana. The Cassana had a large hall capable of holding four thousand people.

Like Shilom, Hanan-Cuzco had many buildings. It also had a "great tower," or fortress, on the hill north of it. Like Nephi, Hurin-Cuzco had a temple and a "tall tower" near the temple. From this tower it would have been possible to overlook the land (city and fields) of Hanan-Cuzco or Shilom. (Mosiah 11:12.)

Plague of Insects

Under king Noah's rule the people became exceedingly wicked. The prophet Abinadi admonished the people to repent or the day would come when they would, "be smitten with the east wind; and insects [would] pester their land . . . and devour their grain." (Mosiah 12:6.)

There is evidence to suggest that such a plague actually happened. South American rivers and lands are often named after an important characteristic or a devastating event. The valley Urubamba (anciently Urupampa) and the river Urubamba (which flows between Cuzco and Pisac — Pisac being about twelve miles east of Cuzco — and which river, in its upper reaches, is called Vilcañota) are examples. (See map, "Original Boundaries of the County Land of Nephi"; see also chapter 6, heading, "The Place of Mormon.") In the Quechua language the word *uru* means caterpillar or grub, while *pampa* means flat land. Therefore, "Urubamba/Urupampa" means "flat-land-where-there-are-grubs-or-caterpillars."[27] Hiram Bingham thought the name of this valley and river strange, for caterpillars and grubs are usually found at a lower elevation. He said, "Only people not accustomed to land where caterpillars and grubs flourished would have been struck by such a circumstance."[27] Garcilaso said that Cuzco's weather is so cool, that "there are no flies, especially in the houses, as well as no mosquitoes, or other disagreeable creatures. . . ."[28]

It seems likely then that hordes of insects, in some such form as butterflies and beetles, invaded that part of the land by coming up from the warm East Sea (Amazon) as Abinadi had prophesied. (Mosiah 12:6.) This could have produced the famine Abinadi predicted. (Mosiah 12:4.) Since the record shows that most of Abinadi's other prophecies were fulfilled, it is no big stretch of imagination to suppose that these were too. It is well to remember that a group of Lamanites, as well as Nephites were living in the county land of Nephi at the time the insects invaded the land. Evidently the Lamanites remembered the incident, which at one time or another may have been repeated, so that through the centuries there has come the echo of the story in the name of "Urubamba," land of the caterpillar and grub.

[27]Bingham, *Lost City of the Incas*, p. 115.
[28]Garcilaso, *The Incas*, p. 212.

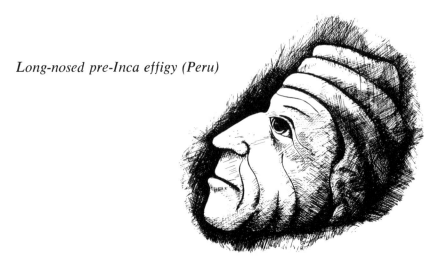

Long-nosed pre-Inca effigy (Peru)

CHAPTER 6

Escape from the Land Nephi

Having in mind the proposed locations of the cities and the terrain involved, it is possible to trace the directional movement of the Nephites and Lamanites who lived in the county land of Nephi. For instance, since king Noah saw the Lamanite warriors moving toward the city of Nephi from the direction of Shemlon (Mosiah 19:6), we conclude from the proposed location of Shemlon that they were coming from the northwest. When their movement was discovered, they were already within the borders of the city land of Nephi, making it impossible for the Nephites to flee to their hilltop fortress (Sacsahuaman), which was north of the city. The tower near the temple, from which king Noah saw the Lamanites coming, adjoined the main square. From there the Antisuyu road ran in an easterly direction. (See chapter 5, heading, "The Land (County) Nephi.") In their flight, Noah and his people logically would have taken this road. From there it was possible to drop down into the Urubamba river

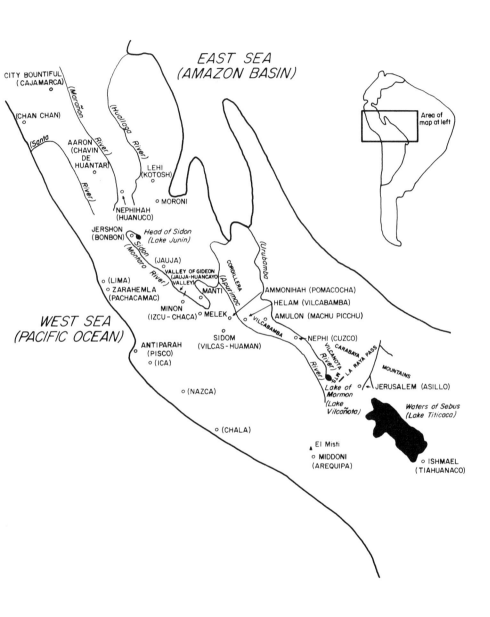

MODERN NAMES OF BOOK OF MORMON LANDS

valley and the Vilcabamba wilderness behind Cuzco (Nephi).[1] (See map, "Original Boundaries of the County Land of Nephi.")

Because the women and children were slower, king Noah "commanded . . . that all the men should leave their wives and their children, and flee before the Lamanites." (Mosiah 19:11.) By following this order many were able to reach safety, possibly in the Vilcabamba wilderness north of Cuzco. Those who remained with their wives and children put themselves at the mercy of the Lamanites and were spared. (Mosiah 19:13-15.) They returned to their homes to live under a heavy Lamanite tax. (Mosiah 19:15.)

The City of Amulon

The wicked priests of Noah, who had safely reached the wilderness, were "ashamed to return to the city of Nephi, yea, and also fearing that the people would slay them, therefore they durst not return to their wives and their children." (Mosiah 20:3.) Thus they retreated into exile.

It appears from Mosiah 20:1-4 that these men moved westward in the wilderness until they were at a position north of the land of Shemlon, whence they moved into the borders of that land and captured twenty-four Lamanite girls. (Mosiah 20:5.) Later they crept into the city of Nephi at night to raid the storehouses and to carry off "grain and many of their precious things." (Mosiah 21:21.) The "precious things" probably included stonecutting instruments and tools for digging and planting. The priests, it seems, had in mind to build a stone city, like the city of Nephi, deep in the Vilcabamba wilderness. (See map, "Escape into Wilderness by Amulon and Fellow Priests.")

About seventy-five miles northwest of Cuzco, at a spot high above the Urubamba river (about 6,750 feet above sea level), are the well-preserved ruins of a stone city called Machu Picchu. When Hiram Bingham discovered Machu

---

[1] As we progressively identify modern lands with Book of Mormon lands, modern and Book of Mormon place names will frequently be used interchangeably in this and later chapters.

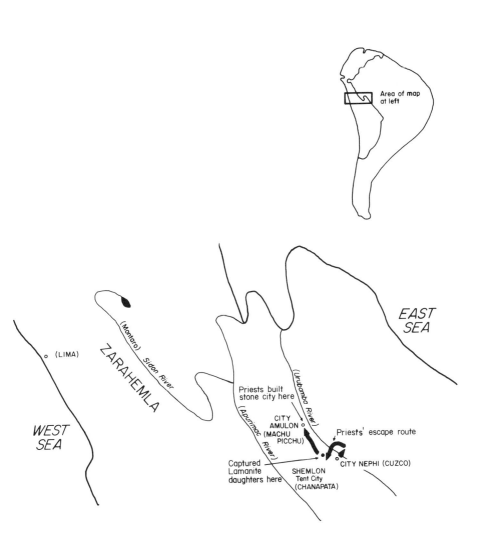

ESCAPE into WILDERNESS
by
AMULON and FELLOW PRIESTS

Picchu he thought he had found the lost Inca city which historians call Vilcabamba the Old, and some authorities still believe that is so. Others place Vilcabamba the Old elsewhere. Interestingly, one tradition has it that in Vilcabamba the Old lived the teachers of idolatry and the masters of evil.[2] Such a description would well fit king Noah's wicked priests. (Mosiah 24:1-4.)

Machu Picchu is said to have been a city which contained everything necessary for living in isolation.[3] It had a good water supply; there were terraces for planting; it had a sundial for telling the hour and the season; and it was well fortified. It stood on a high hill in such a position that the inhabitants could easily keep watch over the valley leading south. This all points to Machu Picchu being Amulon, the city built by Noah's priests.

The Place of Mormon

Previous to the flight of Noah and his priests into the wilderness, Alma, the high priest who believed the words of the prophet Abinadi, "did go forth [with his followers] to a place which was called Mormon, having received its name from the king, being in the borders of the land. . . ." (Mosiah 18:4.) The words "did go forth" mean that the people moved out of the city of Nephi to another place; "in the borders of the land" indicates that they were still within the county land of Nephi.

"Now, there was in Mormon a fountain of pure water. . . ." (Mosiah 18:5), or a clear lake which served as headwaters to a river. It was called by the people the waters (or lake) of Mormon. This lake became of special importance to the people when Alma baptized there.

About seventy-five miles south of Cuzco, at the foot of the Vilcañota knudo (borderline of the county land of Nephi), is a lake called Vilcañota. This lake serves as the headwaters (or "fountain of pure water") for the Vilcañota/

---

[2]Blair Niles, *Peruvian Pageant* (The Bobbs-Merrill Company, Inc., 1964), p. 192.

[3]Hewett, *Ancient Andean Life*, p. 254.

Urubamba river. (Near Cuzco the name of the Vilcañota river changes to Urubamba.) Today, natives of the land call the lake "the sacred lake," and the waters which flow from it, "the sacred river."[4] If Alma once baptized in its waters, that might explain the reverent local name.

When king Noah "discovered a movement among the people" (Mosiah 18:32), he sent spies to find out what was going on. He learned that Alma and his followers were gathering at the waters of Mormon, and he sent troops to destroy them. When the Lord warned Alma of the coming troops, he and his people departed quickly.

Land of Helam

Alma probably would not have ventured further south for fear of being captured as they crossed the Vilcañota knudo. In addition, the land of Helam where Alma and his people settled must have been somewhere in the Vilcabamba wilderness, not many miles from the land of Amulon. (See Mosiah 23:25, 31, 35; see also the section in this chapter headed, "Cities of Amulon and Helam Discovered.")

More than likely Alma and his people fled in a west-northwest direction, possibly using the sound of the Apurimac "Great Speaker" river as a guide. They "fled eight days' journey into the wilderness." (Mosiah 23:3.) An eight-day journey west-northwest of the sacred Vilcañota lake, or a march of approximately 160 miles (twenty miles per day), would have taken them into the Vilcabamba wilderness to a point slightly west and north of Shemlon.

Pinpointed on a National Geographic North-Western South American map (about 160 miles from the Vilcañota lake), are the ruins of an ancient city labeled Vilcabamba. These ruins are only a few miles east of the Apurimac, "Great Speaker," river. (See map, "Alma's Escape to Helam.") The land fits the description of that in which Alma and his people pitched their tents, "a very beautiful and pleasant land, a land of pure water." (Mosiah 23:4.) Through the wild Vilcabamba Cordilleras flow many rivers. In some of

---

[4]Seltzer, *Columbia Lippincott Gazetteer*, p. 1989.

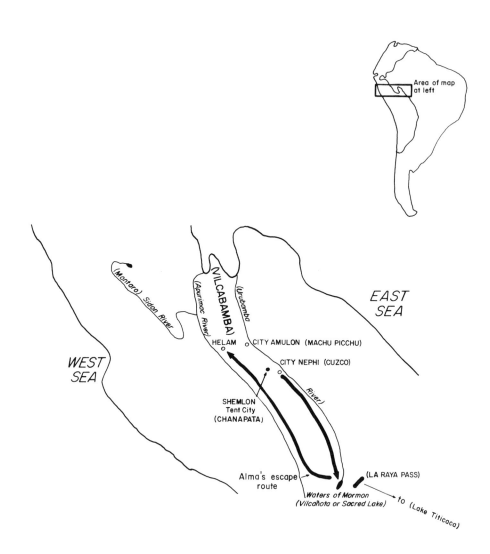

the valleys of the high Andean wilderness there are many tropical plants. Ground orchids, wild strawberries, bamboo plants, sugar cane, begonias and other flowering plants grow in profusion. Some sections of Vilcabamba, though wild, are "very beautiful and pleasant."

Discovery of Jaredite Lands

Leaving Alma and his people in the proposed location for the land of Helam, we move back to the city of Nephi where Noah's son Limhi was now king. The Book of Mormon shows that during king Limhi's reign, Lamanite bondage made life extremely hard for Limhi's people. In desperation, he sent men into the wilderness to seek the land of Zarahemla and deliverance. (Mosiah 8:7.)

As it turned out, the expedition was unsuccessful. The probability of finding a pass through the Andes down to the coast was slim. Even today there are few passes. It is not surprising, then, that the expedition unknowingly passed by the coastal city of Zarahemla, probably less than one hundred miles to the east of it. Instead of finding the land they sought, they traveled northward to as far as Ecuador (see chapters 3 and 4) to a "land among many waters . . . a land which was covered with bones of men, and of beasts. . . ." (Mosiah 8:8.) Here they found twenty-four gold plates which the prophet Ether had hidden. (Ether 15:33.) As a witness that they had found such a land, Limhi's men carried back with them the twenty-four gold plates and some breastplates and swords. (See map, "The Search for the Land of Zarahemla.")

Cities of Amulon and Helam Discovered

Shortly after the return of Limhi's men from the land northward, Ammon, a descendant of Zarahemla, arrived in Nephi along with fifteen other men. (Mosiah 7:2-6.) They had been sent by Mosiah II, king of the Nephite nation in Zarahemla, to check on the welfare of the Nephites in the land of Nephi. It was Ammon who, along with Gideon, finally led king Limhi and his people secretly out of the land of Nephi and out of bondage. They left by way of ". . . the

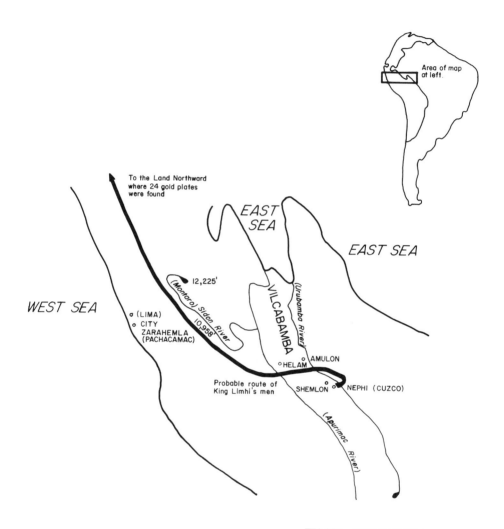

THE SEARCH for the LAND OF ZARAHEMLA

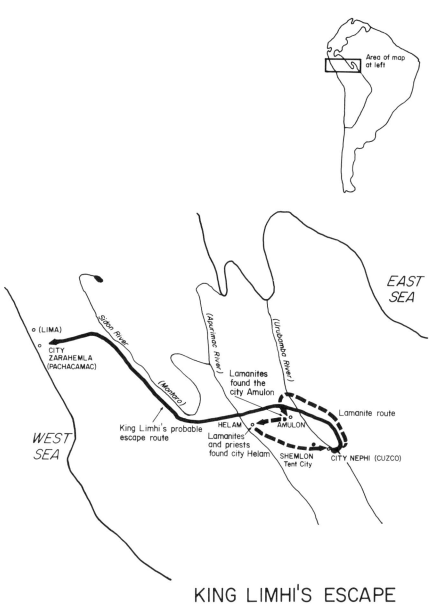

KING LIMHI'S ESCAPE ROUTE

back pass, through the back wall, on the back side of the city." (Mosiah 22:6.) As stated in chapter 5, the back wall was probably the wall of the Sacsahuaman fortress, which can be seen today on the back side of the city of Cuzco. From our knowledge of the terrain we can fill in some of the directional details. They departed by night "and they went round about the land of Shilom . . . and [then] bent their course [in a northwest direction past the land of Amulon and on through the Vilcabamba wilderness] towards the land of Zarahemla. . . ." (Mosiah 22:11.)

Though Limhi's people departed secretly, they left a wide "telltale" trail of escape. The Lamanites pursued them along that trail for two days until "they could no longer follow their tracks; therefore they were lost in the wilderness." (Mosiah 22:16.) It would not be difficult to get lost there. Even today it is easy to become lost in the Vilcabamba wilderness. Some sections are jungle and must be hacked through with machetes. Other sections are open spaces of soft black mud covered with dry moss. Still other sections are covered with tall grass. Others are too boggy to traverse. During the Lamanites' frantic search in this wilderness for the way back to the city of Nephi, they accidentally stumbled across the city of Amulon. (Mosiah 23:30-31.)

Amulon and his fellow priests joined the Lamanites, and together they took up the search for the city of Nephi. But the priests were not much help, for they too lost their way. When the combined group discovered the land of Helam (assuming our proposed locations for Amulon and Helam are correct) they were off course nearly 120°. Alma had to show them the way back to the city of Nephi. (Mosiah 23:35-37.)

People of Alma Escape

Because of their superior numbers and aggressive intent, the Lamanites and priests placed the people of Helam under bondage. From that time forth Alma and his people cried continually to the Lord for deliverance. (Mosiah 24:10.) In answer to their great faith and prayers the Lord finally

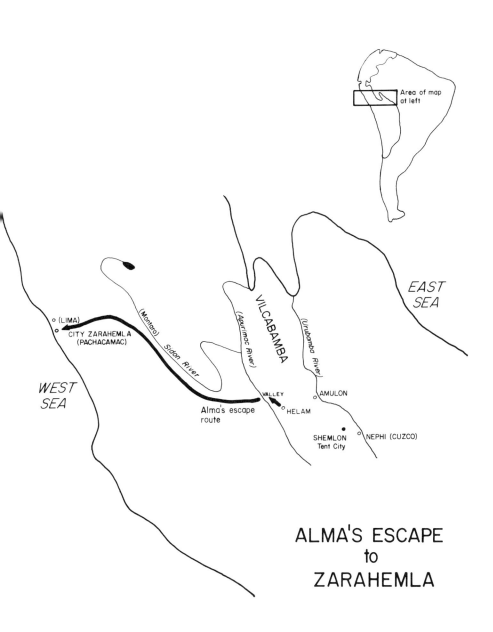

told Alma, ". . . on the morrow I will deliver you out of bondage." (Mosiah 24:16.) In great haste Alma and his people began to gather their flocks and grains; ". . . even all the night-time were they gathering their flocks together. And in the morning the Lord caused a deep sleep to come upon the Lamanites, yea, and all their task-masters were in a profound sleep." (Mosiah 24:18-19.)

Today's name for the land in which Alma and his people built their city Helam is Vilcabamba or Vilacampa, meaning "valley of the narcotic berry."[5] A powder is made from the seeds of the narcotic plant to be used as snuff, and it produces a kind of hypnotic state. Could the sleeping Lamanites in Helam have in some way come under the influence of the narcotic berry?

Alma and his people traveled all day, then "pitched their tents in a valley. . . ." (Mosiah 24:20.) More than likely the valley was on the east banks of the "Great Speaker" river.

Now the Lord said to Alma: "Haste thee and get thou and this people out of this land, for the Lamanites have awakened and do pursue thee; therefore get thee out of this land, and I will stop the Lamanites in this valley that they come no further in pursuit of this people." (Mosiah 24:23.)

Could the Lord have been saying, "Hurry and cross the river"? The deep, perilous Apurimac river did not stop the Nephites, yet the Lord could have caused it to stop the Lamanites. The Apurimac or "Great Speaker" river will rise more than fifty feet during a heavy rainstorm. Often such a rise will take place quickly.[6]

---

[5]Beals, *Nomads and Empire Builders*, p. 234.
[6]Bingham, *Lost City of the Incas*, p. 101.

Feather-headed staff of Inca nobleman (Peru)

CHAPTER 7

Zarahemla

"And after they had been in the wilderness twelve days they arrived in the land of Zarahemla. . . ." (Mosiah 24:25.) An average of twenty miles a day would not be unreasonable for a hardy people accustomed to such territory and in flight from a ferocious enemy. This would have taken them a distance of about 240 miles, bringing them from the place of their river crossing to today's Pachacamac.

Pachacamac is located about twenty miles south of Lima, Peru, in the Lurin-Ramic river valley. It is near the mouth of the Lurin river, about one-half mile back from the sea.

Archaeologists say that this large city was once an ancient cultural center or "Mecca" for South America. Scholars of the Quechua language say that the meaning of the name *Pachacamac* is that God dwelt there. That is very close to the idea that the Prophet, Seer, and Revelator dwelt there. Zarahemla was the home of Benjamin, Mosiah, Alma, Helaman, and other prophets and seers.

Pizarro's secretary, Estete, wrote that Pachacamac ". . .

has been surrounded by a wall, though now most of it has fallen."¹ Zarahemla of course was surrounded by a wall. Samuel the Lamanite preached from the wall of Zarahemla. (Helaman 13:4.) And "many . . . heard the words of Samuel, the Lamanite, which he spake upon the walls of the city." (Helaman 16:1.) The area enclosed by Pachacamac's walls was approximately 2½ by 1½ miles, or 2,420 acres.²

Pachacamac (Zarahemla) had straight streets, large plazas, storehouses, baths, a great pyramid called the Sun Temple, and a smaller temple called the Temple of Pachacamac or the Temple of God. The ruins of Pachacamac or Zarahemla are scattered over several hills, and upon the highest hill sits the remains of the Temple of the Sun. At the northern base of the Sun Temple are the ruins of the Temple of God or the Temple of Pachacamac. It measures 400 feet in length and 180 feet in width.³

Like the city itself, the Temple of God or of Pachacamac was surrounded by walls. They were of thick sun-dried adobe. E. L. Hewett wrote: "The temple was in a large enclosure, heavily walled, and seems to have been well isolated. . . ."⁴

The Book of Mormon wording indicates that the temple at Zarahemla was on a hill, since the people had to go "up to the temple" (Mosiah 2:5) to hear king Benjamin speak. Likewise it was enclosed by a wall; for when the people had "pitched their tents round about the temple . . . [there were so many people that] king Benjamin could not teach them all within the walls of the temple, therefore he caused a tower to be erected [higher than the temple walls], that thereby his people might hear [his] words. . . ." (Mosiah 2:6-7.)

The Land (County) Zarahemla

Some twenty years after Alma arrived in the city of Zarahemla the people began to settle lands ". . . on the north

---
¹Niles, *Peruvian Pageant*, p. 62.
²Hewett, *Ancient Andean Life*, p. 228.
³Hewett, *Ancient Andean Life*, pp. 228-229.
⁴Hewett, *Ancient Andean Life*, p. 230.

and on the south, on the east and on the west, building large cities and villages in all quarters of the land." (Mosiah 27:6.)

It appears that the northern boundaries of the land Zarahemla were around Paramonga, about 110 miles north of Lima. (The land Bountiful was north of that point.) The southern boundaries apparently were near Pisco, about 120 miles south of Lima. (Lamanite territory started south of there and continued all the way down through Chile and what is now part of Argentina.) The eastern boundaries of the county land of Zarahemla were along the Montaro or Sidon river, about 100 miles east of Lima. (Land to the east of the Sidon river was called the South Wilderness.) People also settled along the coast near Pachacamac. In all these places they built "large cities and villages." (Mosiah 27:6.)

Notice that the land (county) of Zarahemla was roughly oblong in shape and that the Montaro or Sidon river, "ran by the [eastern borders of the] land of Zarahemla." (Alma 2:15.) Notice too that the city of Zarahemla was in "the heart of their lands." (Helaman 1:18; Alma 60:19.) (See map, "Zarahemla and the Sidon River.")

Sidon River

The course of the Montaro river (Sidon) is important to Book of Mormon geography and some comments on this river are therefore appropriate. The Montaro river is not particularly useful to man. As with many other rivers in the high Andes, great forces of moving waters have here scored out a canyon so deep that man has been unable to harness the river for his benefit. Victor von Hagen said of this river: "The Montaro must, like unreasonable weather, be endured. Yet, the Incas refused to endure it — they avoided it. . . they laid their communication system [road] above it and out of harm's way."[5]

Unlike other rivers which start as a trickle or small brook, the river Montaro (Sidon) bursts forth from Lake Junin (waters of Sidon) fullborn, and within fifty miles it

---

[5]Von Hagen, *Highway of the Sun*, p. 161.

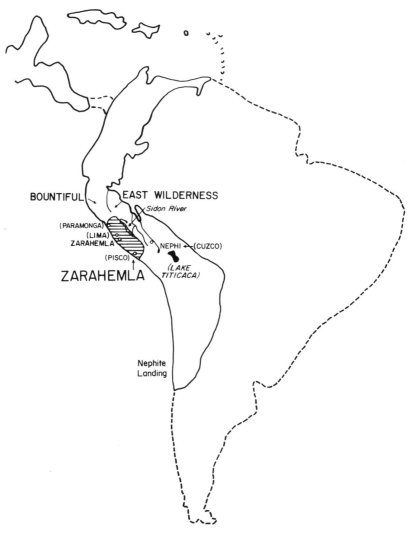

ZARAHEMLA
and the
SIDON RIVER

is an earthmoving force.[6] It flows south from Lake Junin for a distance of about 160 miles, makes a fishhook turn eastward (very important in Nephite geography), and then feeds into the Apurimac or "Great Speaker" river. Interestingly enough it is as large in the Andes at twelve thousand feet as the Hudson river is near its mouth.[7]

Some have felt that, during the judgments poured out in A.D. 34 when "the whole face of the land was changed" (3 Nephi 8:12), the river Sidon changed also, perhaps even disappeared. Yet to judge from Mormon's comment three hundred years later, the river remained in his day, as did many cities and towns. He tells us that "war began . . . in the borders of Zarahemla, by the waters of Sidon." (Mormon 1:10.) It is reasonable then to believe that the Sidon is still flowing and that it follows the same course it always has.

Valley of Gideon

Traces are still found of an ancient Incan lateral road which ran up through the rugged Andes from Pachacamac (Zarahemla) to the river Montaro (Sidon). A suspension bridge at Jauja continued that road to the east side of the river, where it joined with the main highway system. From that place the sound of war was heard throughout the land. Amlici, a high-spirited, aggressive man, had mustered his troops "upon the hill Amnihu, which was east of the river Sidon . . . ," and from that point he "began to make war with the Nephites." (Alma 2:15.) At this, Alma ". . . went up [into the Andes] with his people . . . to battle." (Alma 2:16.) The defeated Amlicites fled through the valley of Gideon. (Alma 2:20.)

Today's Jauja-Huancayo valley, which moves southward from Jauja and parallels the Montaro river for a distance of about fifty miles, must surely have been the valley of Gideon. About twenty miles south of the suspension bridge at Jauja, in the Jauja-Huancayo valley, is today's city of Huancayo. More than likely this city was the ancient city of Gideon.

---

[6]Von Hagen, *Highway of the Sun*, p. 161.
[7]Beals, *Nomads and Empire Builders*, p. 31.

A later reference says that Alma "went over [indicating that he went from the coast into the Andes] upon the east of the river Sidon, into the valley of Gideon [Jauja-Huancayo valley], there having been a city built, which was called the city of Gideon, which was in the valley that was called Gideon. . . ." (Alma 6:7.) At the city of Huancayo today the road widens through this 10,731-foot valley to about three times its normal width. Periodically a colorful market is held here.

South of the valley of Gideon the Inca road divided, one division moving southeast, the other southwest. Amlici must have taken the southwest road which crossed over the river Sidon to the west bank at Izcu-Chaca.

Alma followed Amlici's army, and "when [he] could pursue the Amlicites no longer he caused that his people should pitch their tents in the valley of Gideon. . . ." (Alma 2:20.)

"And Alma sent spies to follow the . . . Amlicites . . . and to . . . [their] astonishment, in the land of Minon . . . [they] saw a numerous host of the Lamanites; and . . . the Amlicites . . . joined them." (Alma 2:21, 24.)

Minon

About forty-five miles north of the Montaro's great fishhook curve, on the west side of the Montaro (Sidon) at today's Izcu-Chaca, is the possible land of Minon. This location fits the Book of Mormon location, i.e., ". . . above the land [city] of Zarahemla, in the course of [or along the road to] the land of Nephi. . . ." (Alma 2:24.)

From the fact that the elevation of the Andes at that place is about eleven thousand feet, and that it drops to about sea level in less than one hundred miles, we can visualize the ruggedness and steepness of the land. In order to reach Zarahemla quickly the Amlicites, as well as the Nephites, needed an easy pass down to the city of Zarahemla. This pass would have been at Jauja, where a lateral road moved down from the Andes to the coast. The Amlicites knew the road well, and they hurried toward it with their Lamanite allies

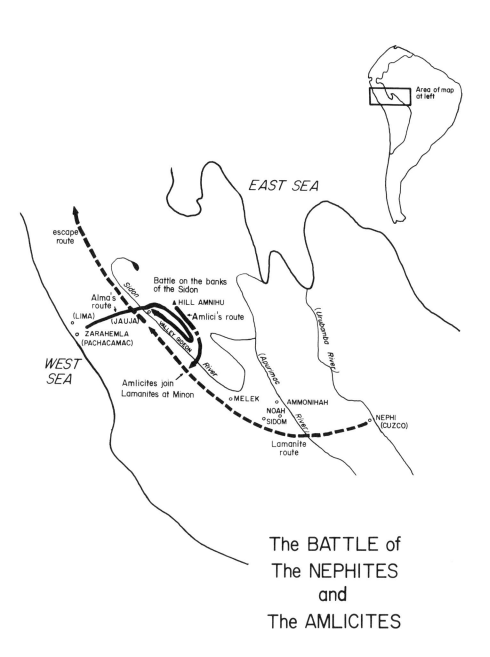

The BATTLE of
The NEPHITES
and
The AMLICITES

along the west side of the river Sidon. Meantime the Nephites hurried toward it on the east side of the river.

Alma and his people arrived at Jauja only seconds before the Lamanites reached the opposite point on the west side of the river; and ". . . as they were crossing [to the west side of] the river Sidon [by way of the suspension bridge], the Lamanites and the Amlicites . . . came upon them. . . ." (Alma 2:27.) The problem was that only a portion of Alma's troops had crossed to the west side before the fighting began. Many were stopped midway on the bridge because of the great masses of fighting men, as well as dead bodies, which clogged the bridge. During a lull in the fighting, Alma and his guards "cleared the ground, or rather the bank, which was on the west of the river Sidon, throwing the bodies of the Lamanites who had been slain into the waters of Sidon, that thereby [the rest of] his people might have room to cross and contend with the Lamanites and the Amlicites on the west side of the river Sidon." (Alma 2:34.) (See map, "The Battle of the Nephites and the Amlicites.")

Hermounts

Faced now with the entire Nephite army, the Lamanites and Amlicites fled. For some unexplained reason (perhaps because the Nephites had cut off that route) they did not go the way they had come. Rather they fled "towards the wilderness which was west and north, away beyond the borders of the [county] land [of Zarahemla]; . . . until they had reached the wilderness, which was called Hermounts; and it was that part of the wilderness which was infested by wild and ravenous beasts." (Alma 2:35-37.) I suggest that Hermounts was somewhere south of Loja, Ecuador, and north of Paramonga. Hermounts was "beyond the borders of the land [of Zarahemla]," which would have placed it in the land of Bountiful. (See chapter 9, heading "The Land [County] Bountiful.")

The one-hundred-mile stretch of land directly north of Paramonga is sandy and dry. A Spaniard quaintly described it as "a land full of dispeoplement." Victor von Hagen said that the only thing Inca along that stretch was the road. These are good indications that this part of the land was a Nephite wilderness, perhaps even the wilderness of Hermounts.

Melek and Ammonihah

Alma gave up his judgment seat so that he might preach the gospel to the people. He traveled ". . . over into the land of Melek, on the west [side] of the river Sidon, on the west by the borders of the wilderness." (Alma 8:3.) It is important to remember that the north-south Inca road did not cross over to the west side of the Montaro (Sidon) river until it divided into two roads (see section headed "Minon") south of the valley of Gideon (Jauja-Huancayo valley). Being on the west of the river and near the wilderness, Melek must have been south of the land of Minon at the place where the river Montaro begins its great turn, and where the previously divided road once again becomes one. In that area today is a place called Mayoc. Mayoc could easily have been Melek.

From Melek Alma "departed thence, and traveled three days' journey on the north of the land Melek. . . ." (Alma 8:6.) Notice that the recorder said "on the north" and not "to the north" of the land Melek. Three days' journey "to the north" of our proposed location of Melek, at about twenty miles a day, sixty miles total, would have taken Alma back to Huancayo, our proposed land and city of Gideon. Therefore, "on the north" could mean that Alma traveled along the northern borders of Melek, either to the east or to the west. Had he journeyed to the west he would have moved down the steep western side of the Andes mountains toward Zarahemla, which was in the heart of the land. But Ammonihah was in the borders of the land (". . . the armies of the Lamanites had come in upon the wilderness side, into the borders of the land, even into the city of Ammonihah" — Alma 16:2). Therefore it appears that he traveled eastward from the city of Melek.

About sixty miles eastward from Mayoc (Melek) in the southeastern quarter of the proposed county land of Zarahemla are the ruins of Pomacocha — more correctly Puman-Chochan, "Lake of the Lion." These ruins are unique in that they lay in what Victor von Hagen said "seemed to be the bottom of a volcano."[8] The stone city and small shallow lake were completely surrounded by a rim of the supposed crater of the volcano. A forty-five-foot-wide road moved through a broken lip of the ridge.

After Alma's visit Ammonihah was destroyed by the Lamanites. Years later a new group of people came to inhabit that city and they ". . . cast up dirt . . ." (Alma 49:2) and ". . . dug up a ridge of earth round about them, which was so high that the Lamanites could not cast their stones and their arrows at them . . . neither could they come upon them save it was by their place of entrance." (Alma 49:4.) To build a "ridge of earth" so high that it resembled the "rim of a crater" may sound like an impossible job; yet, when considering the hundreds of miles of terraces that line the sides of the mountains in Peru, it does not seem too unreasonable a task. In order to understand how this could be, perhaps a brief description of terrace-building would be in order here.

Stones were used to construct retaining walls sometimes fifteen or twenty feet high, behind which other stones were laid to form a level bed. Subsoil, or small coarse stones and clay, were then packed on that bed to within two or three feet of the top of the retaining wall. Over the subsoil, topsoil was laid. Mountain terraces often climbed in steps of fifty or more, each step often being from eight to fifteen feet wide and several hundred feet long. Some have suggested that soil to fill the terraces was carried many miles on the backs of the farmers. With the same persistence as used in the terrace-building, a ridge resembling the "rim of a crater" could have been formed.

Victor von Hagen said: "Nowhere outside of the Cuzco area had we seen such magnificent stonework nor such precision in filling. . . . Smaller stones combined with large ones were so interlocked that the walls were actually a stone mosaic. . . ."[9] Could it have been that some of Limhi's people, disliking the coastal area, moved to the Andean

---

[8]Von Hagen, *Highway of the Sun*, p. 153.
[9]Von Hagen, *Highway of the Sun*, p. 156.

highlands and founded Ammonihah, carrying there the skills in stonecutting and building which they had already exhibited in the city of Nephi (Cuzco)?

The ruins revealed a palace whose foundations projected slightly into the lake. There was also a large fountain or bath, terraces, and a sundial.[10]

Sidom

Alma and his companion Amulek, the lawyer Zeezrom, and others were forced to leave the city Ammonihah, "and they departed, and came out even into the land of Sidom. . . ." (Alma 15:1.)

Vilcas-Huaman, or the "Sanctuary of the Hawk," is relatively close to Pomacocha on a high, horseshoe-shaped plateau — elevation about eleven thousand feet. Vilcas-Huaman could boast both a Sun Temple and a palace the size of a square city block. Vilcas-Huaman was close enough to Pomacocha to have been the logical city in which to take sanctuary. It could easily have been Sidom.

Manti and the South Wilderness

After Ammonihah was destroyed, other cities from surrounding territories were sacked and many Nephites were taken "captive into the wilderness." (Alma 16:4.) Alma informed the Nephite military leaders that the Lamanites, with their prisoners, would "cross the river Sidon in the south wilderness, away up beyond the borders of the land of Manti. And . . . there shall ye meet them, on the east of the river Sidon. . . ." (Alma 16:6.)

The above scripture gives the idea that Manti was east of the river Sidon. Further direction is given in Alma 17:1, where it is learned that Manti was south of Gideon; "Alma was journeying from the land of Gideon southward, away to the land of Manti. . . ." "Away to the land of Manti" probably meant that Alma turned eastward where the Inca road divided at the southern end of the valley of Gideon (westward would have taken him to Minon). It is remembered

---

[10]Von Hagen, *Highway of the Sun,* pp. 156-157.

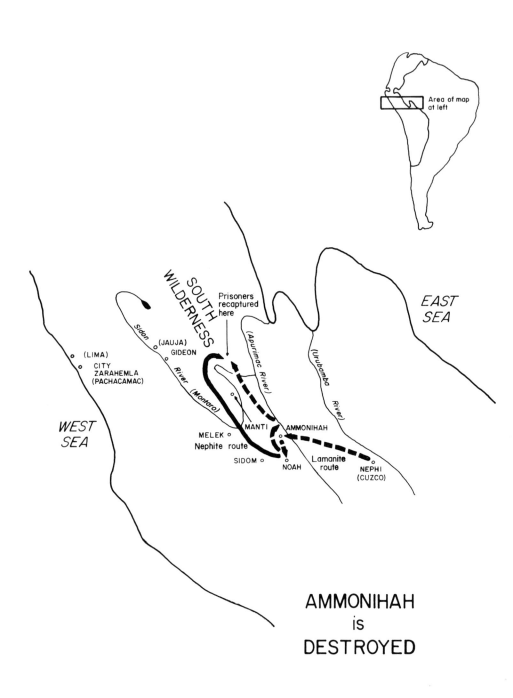

that Gideon was "east of the river Sidon" (Alma 6:7), again strengthening the idea that Manti was east of the Sidon. If the proposed location for Ammonihah is correct, Manti was north of Ammonihah. But Manti was also west of the river Sidon, since Moroni concealed part of his army "in the west valley, on the west of the river Sidon, and so down into the borders of the land Manti." (Alma 43:32.) This may sound confusing until it is realized that Manti rested in the fishhook curve of the Sidon (Montaro) river.

Look at the accompanying map, "Ammonihah is Destroyed." Notice that the South Wilderness was "east of the river Sidon" and "away up beyond the borders of the land Manti." Manti itself was both west and east of the Sidon, away from the main road or highway which led southward from Gideon. Traces of the road that Alma may have traveled to Manti are there. Also there are the valley and the river, with Inca ruins located at various points along the river. All this lends credence to the belief that the Montaro river and no other is the Sidon river.

Part IV
From Ishmael to Cumorah

Tiahuanaco costume (Lake Titicaca area)

CHAPTER 8

Anti-Nephi-Lehi

The sons of Mosiah left Zarahemla "to go up to the land of Nephi, to preach the word of God unto the Lamanites." (Alma 17:8.)

When they arrived in Lamanite territory, Ammon blessed his companions and sent them on their various ways. (Alma 17:13, 18.) He continued southward until he came to the land of Ishmael — apparently at the southern end of Lake Titicaca.

Land and City of Ishmael

It appears that what is today called Tiahuanaco was the land Ishmael. In Quechua, *Tiahuanaco* means "the place of the dead" or "the place of those who were."[1] This gives the impression that a great exodus must have taken place from that city. Archaeologists say that such a thing did happen. "It is as though the entire civilization . . . had descended upon the spot from another world and, as myster-

---

[1]Verrill and Verrill, *America's Ancient Civilizations*, p. 200.

iously as they had arrived, had returned from whence they came."[2] (Alma 27:12.) A. Hyatt and Ruth Verrill said that the work on the buildings of Tiahuanaco was never finished. "For some unknown reason the city was abandoned before the greatest buildings had been completed. Everything was halted, all work stopped and Tiahuanaco was deserted."[3]

Ammon and his missionary companions were instrumental in converting many Lamanites who immediately "began to be a very industrious people" (Alma 23:18), whereas previously they had been "a very indolent people" (Alma 17:15). Undoubtedly one target of their new-found energies would have been the beautification of their cities, including the erection of civic and religious buildings. These would all have been commenced within a very few years — then abandoned, many of them unfinished, when the people left the land under Ammon's leadership to save their lives from the unconverted Amalekite/Amulonite-led Lamanites.[4] Ishmael apparently was one such city. (See Alma 23:8-9.) To the explorer of two thousand years later its ruins would indeed suggest a civilization which arrived suddenly and then departed as mysteriously as it had come.

During the years Ammon lived there the city and land of Ishmael must have been at a much lower elevation than was the city and land of Nephi. The Lord told Ammon, "Thou shalt not go up to the land of Nephi." (Alma 20:2.) The Tiahuanaco plains are much higher today. Immanuel Velikovsky has reported that "the last upheaval . . . [of the Andes mountains] took place in an early historical period, after the city of Tiahuanaco had been built. . . ."[5]

---

[2]Verrill and Verrill, *America's Ancient Civilizations*, pp. 199-200.

[3]Verrill and Verrill, *America's Ancient Civilization*, p. 208.

[4]Recall that Amulon and his brethren were made teachers in every Lamanite land. (Mosiah 24:4.) Besides teaching the language of Nephi (Mosiah 24:4), writing and record keeping (Mosiah 24:6), could it be that they also taught the art of stonecutting? (145-123 B.C.) Before Ammon arrived in the land of Ishmael (about 90 B.C.), the Lamanites were building "Towers of the Dead" or sepulchres. (Alma 19:1.) These stone towers may still be seen standing in various places around Lake Titicaca. (See section headed "Towers of the Dead.")

[5]Immanuel Velikovsky, *Earth in Upheaval* (New York: Doubleday and Co., 1955), p. 84.

Today the Tiahuanaco plain is about 12,500 feet high. Man-made terraces on the surrounding mountains rise to heights of 15,000 feet and some higher still to "18,400 feet above sea level, or to the present line of eternal snow."[6]

Agricultural terraces which reach to heights of over 18,000 feet are unthinkable. Even the hardy potato will grow only to heights of about 15,000 feet. This fact makes it clear that Tiahuanaco formerly was at least 3,400 feet lower than it is today. Its elevation would then have been about 9,100 feet.

"Radiocarbon dating of materials from Tiahuanaco indicate the site is much younger than expected. The early classic style there is dated to about the fifth century B.C., and the following cultural period to about the time of Christ. (Ref. Radiocarbon Vol. IV 1962, p. 91) . . . It would seem from these dates that the geological upheavals . . . came very late. This is in agreement with the impression of Darwin, for example, that the uplift of the South American coast was very recent. . . . The terraces [at Tiahuanaco] are not quite horizontal but rise to the south."[7]

Waters of Sebus

Ammon found favor in the eyes of king Lamoni by contending with dangerous renegades while watering the king's flocks at the waters of Sebus. (Alma 17:26-39.)

The waters of Sebus, in all probability, were the waters of Lake Titicaca. The ruins of Tiahuanaco, our proposed city of Ishmael, are about thirteen miles south of the lake. Yet north of the city there are traces of what appears to be a dock. This dock has led archaeologists to believe that at one time the shores of Lake Titicaca, or an arm of that lake, brought the waters to the north of the city.[8] This belief fits very well with the story of Ammon tending the king's flocks at the waters of Sebus.

---

[6]Velikovsky, *Earth in Upheaval*, p. 82.
[7]Charles H. Hapgood, *The Path of the Pole* (Philadelphia: Chilton Book Co., 1970), pp. 286, 365. Copyright © 1970 by the author. Used with permission.
[8]Verrill, *Old Civilizations of the New World*, p. 260.

Towers of the Dead

Ammon was able to teach king Lamoni the gospel. Upon accepting Ammon's teachings, the king was overcome by the Spirit and fell to the ground as if he were dead. Many thought he was dead. After two days in a coma it was suggested ". . . that he ought to be placed in the sepulchre. . . ." (Alma 19:5.) "And . . . they were about to take his body and lay it in a sepulchre, which they had made for the purpose of burying their dead." (Alma 19:1.)

Sepulchres, called by archaeologists "Towers of the Dead," are found in various places around Lake Titicaca and in the Carabaya mountains. Some are round and others square. All have a low narrow doorway and no windows. They rise to a height of about fourteen feet. The towers were built of perfectly cut stones put together without mortar.

Not far from Tiahuanaco, at Qutimbo, there are so many towers that it gives the appearance of a great stone forest. Victor von Hagen said: "We came to the forest of Chullpas. As far as we could see there was nothing to relieve the eye except these stone burial towers."[9]

Anti-Nephi-Lehies

After king Lamoni's conversion, he and the other converts wished to "have a name, that thereby they might be distinguished from their brethren . . ." (Alma 23:16.) They therefore took upon themselves the name Anti-Nephi-Lehies. The prefix "Anti" before "Nephi-Lehi" has puzzled many Book of Mormon readers, perhaps because they had always associated the names Nephi and Lehi with the Nephites rather than with the Lamanites.

Study the map "The Original Land of Nephi" in chapter 5 of this book. Notice which lands were possessed by the Lamanites at the time the sons of Mosiah took their journey into those lands. Modern Chile, to as far north as the Titicaca basin, was called the land of Lehi, and was possessed by the Lamanites. "Now the land south [not the land southward,

---

[9]Von Hagen, *Highway of the Sun*, p. 46.

for there is a difference] was called Lehi . . . for the Lord did bring . . . Lehi into the land south" (Helaman 6:10), meaning the southern section of the land southward.[10]

The Cuzco basin of course was the land of Nephi. "And my people would that we should call the name of the place Nephi; wherefore, we did call it Nephi." (2 Nephi 5:8.) When the Lamanites took possession of the land of Nephi they added the prefix *Lehi t*o signify their possession of the land. Thus the land of Nephi became known as the land of Lehi-Nephi. The city of Nephi likewise became known as the city of Lehi-Nephi. (Mosiah 9:6, 8.) We may conclude that the name Nephi was by association given to the Lamanites living in the land of Lehi-Nephi, just as the name Lehi probably was accepted by those living in the land of Lehi further south. On this assumption, those in Lehi would presumably have been known as Lehies, and those in the former land of Nephi as Nephies.

Anti means against; opposed in opinions, sympathy, or practice. The converts to the Church who wished to distinguish themselves from their unconverted brethren called themselves "Anti" (opposed to the old traditions) "Nephi-Lehies" (those who lived in the lands of Nephi and Lehi). That is, they called themselves Anti-Nephi-Lehies.

When the converted Lamanites left these lands (Alma 23:8-12) and established themselves in the land of Jershon they became known as the people of Ammon. (Alma 27:26.)

Middoni

Middoni was lower in altitude than both Nephi and Ishmael. We draw this conclusion from Lamoni's words to Ammon, "I will go with thee down to the land of Middoni. . . ." (Alma 20:7), and from the Lamanite king's later desire to "know the cause why [Ammon] has not come up out of Middoni. . . ." (Alma 22:3). Middoni must have been on the coast, for it was said that ". . . they departed and came

---

[10]The northern section of the land southward, or the land north, was called Mulek. (Helaman 6:10.) This included Zarahemla, Bountiful and the East Wilderness. (See Introduction.)

over into the land of Middoni." (Alma 21:12.) Bear in mind that the terms "came over," "come over," and "went over" usually referred to a trip from the Andes to the coast or vice versa.

In all probability Middoni was near today's Arequipa. And what better place to build a city in that area than in the shadow of the slim 19,098-foot El Misti!

Jerusalem

Ammon's missionary brethren had many hard experiences while in the land of Lehi-Nephi. Aaron first came to the land of Jerusalem, which "was away joining the borders of Mormon." (Alma 21:1.) This could have been south of the LaRaya pass, at the entrance to the Carabaya country. The Carabaya was close enough to Mormon for it to have been said that their borders joined. (Alma 21:1.) While no other geographical description is given of Jerusalem, it probably was near today's Asillo, not far from a swift-flowing stream.

Victor von Hagen speaks of a lake at Asillo. He said that the Inca built this city high on a hill to be out of reach of the lake's periodic overflow.[11] The inhabitants of Jerusalem were buried in the earth when Christ was crucified, after which, the Lord said, "waters have I caused to come up in the stead thereof, to hide their wickedness . . . from before my face. . . ." (3 Nephi 9:7.) The phrase "waters have I caused to come up" perhaps indicates that lake waters flowed in to cover the sunken city. It may well be then that the ruins of Jerusalem are in the lake near today's Asillo.

Leaving Jerusalem and the village of Ani-Anti, Aaron "came over" to Middoni, where he was thrown into prison. (Alma 21:11-13.) After his release, Aaron went to the land of Nephi (Hurin-Cuzco) to preach to the Lamanite king. (Alma 22:1.) The king accepted the word of God and "sent a proclamation among all his people, that they [the people] should not lay their hands on [the Nephite missionaries] . . . who should go forth preaching . . . in any part of their land." (Alma 23:1.)

---

[11]Von Hagen, *Highway of the Sun,* p. 59.

King's Lands

A description of the king's lands is found in Alma 22:27-33. The accompanying map, entitled "King's Lands," shows the locations of these lands as they are there described.

A word must be said here about Alma 22:30-31, which reads as follows: "And it [Bountiful] bordered upon the land which they called Desolation, it being so far northward that it came into the land which had been peopled and been destroyed, of whose bones we have spoken, which was discovered by the people of Zarahemla, it being the place of their first landing. And they came from there up into the south wilderness. Thus the land on the northward was called Desolation, and the land on the southward was called Bountiful, it being the wilderness which is filled with all manner of wild animals of every kind, a part of which had come from the land northward for food."

Interpretations of these verses can differ, depending on how one relates pronouns to antecedents. It could mean that the Mulekites discovered the land of the Jaredites' battleground (or a nearby land) after landing, and came from there into the south wilderness, presumably on their way south to Zarahemla, where they would then remain permanently. (Omni 16.) It could instead mean that the land of Desolation, or the land bordering it, was the place where the Jaredites first landed and that they later came south into the South Wilderness to hunt, as indicated by Ether 10:21. The latter interpretation seems to me the more likely one, and the map reflects that position. Note that this gives us two south wildernesses — that of the Jaredites, south of Desolation, and that of the Nephites, which was south of the East Wilderness.

Jershon

It became clear that if the people of Anti-Nephi-Lehi remained in Lamanite lands they would all be slaughtered by their enemies. For this reason the Lord said to Ammon, "Get this people out of this land, that they perish not. . . ." (Alma 27:12.) Accordingly, all the people who were called

Anti-Nephi-Lehies gathered together and left the land in one large body. They moved into the narrow strip of "wilderness which divided the land of Nephi from the land of Zarahemla. . . ." (Alma 27:14.) (See map, "King's Lands.") They waited in this no-man's-land while Ammon and his brethren traveled into Zarahemla to see if the Nephites would accept the Lamanite immigrants.

The answer was yes. The Nephite people said, "We will give up the land of Jershon, which is on the east by the sea. . . ." (Alma 27:22.) "East by the sea" does not necessarily mean the East Sea. Our scribe makes this clear when he explains that the sea ". . . joins the land Bountiful, which [sea] is on the south of the land Bountiful. . . ." (Alma 27:22.) Lake Junin is east of Zarahemla and south of the land Bountiful. Zarahemla's Lake Junin apparently was considered an inland sea by the Nephites in much the same way as the Lake of Galilee was considered a sea by the Israelites.

Look at the map. Notice that the river Montaro (Sidon) flows north from the lake, makes a "U" turn, and then pushes south about 160 miles before it swings into its great fishhook turn. On the west side of Lake Junin, tucked up in the river's "U" loop, are the ruins of an ancient city called Bonbon. I feel certain that Bonbon was Jershon.

Notice how the lake would have protected Bonbon or Jershon on its east side. Lake Junin is about twenty-five miles long and eight to ten miles wide. The swift, deep river Montaro (Sidon) flowing from Junin protected the city on the north and on the west. A suspension bridge was the only means by which one coming from those directions could cross over the river.

The southern section was the only place open to possible attack. "We will give up the land of Jershon," the Nephites said. "And . . . we will set our armies between the land Jershon and the land Nephi, that we may protect our brethren in the land of Jershon. . . ." (Alma 27:22-23.) Since the Lamanite lands basically were south of the Nephite lands, this statement must mean that the Nephites would put their armies to the south of Jershon. Protected by natural obstacles from attacks on the other three sides, the newcomers would be secure.

The city of Bonbon or Jershon had an immense plaza which was about a thousand feet long. In the center stood the Sun Temple. There were, in Bonbon, about five hundred stone structures.[12] These buildings might well have been built by those thousands of "very industrious people" (Alma 23:18), the converted Lamanites.

---

[12]Von Hagen, *Highway of the Sun,* pp. 183-184.

War club (Peru)

CHAPTER 9
Nephite War Zones

"Now the Zoramites had gathered themselves together in a land which they called Antionum, which was east of the land of Zarahemla, which lay nearly bordering upon the seashore, which was south of the land of Jershon, which also bordered upon the wilderness south. . . ." (Alma 31:3.)

The "seashore" referred to here, as discussed in the previous chapter, was the shore of Lake Junin. From the army movements resulting from the Zoramites' defection (see below) it appears that Antionum was twenty-fives miles or so from Jershon, in a generally southerly direction, at the southern end of the lake.

Following Alma's partial missionary success in their land, the unrepentant Zoramites were angry with the people of Ammon, and they joined the Lamanites with the intent of attacking Jershon. (Alma 35:8, 10-11.) The people of Ammon moved out of Jershon and over to Melek (verse 13), at the southernmost end of the river, and the Nephite army moved into the vacated land to be ready to meet the enemy in that area. The combined army of Lamanites (some of whom were Amalekites) "with their thousands" (Alma 43:5) and traitorous Zoramites (verse 4) was led by Zoramite and Amalekite chief captains (verse 6).

Moroni's First Stratagem

Moroni had command of the Nephite army. That army not only had offensive weapons but also thick clothing, breastplates, arm-shields, and shields for their heads. Since the native Lamanites were nearly naked, their captains, on seeing the Nephites' protective armor, decided not to attack. Instead their army "departed out of the land of Antionum into the wilderness, and took their journey round about in the wilderness, away by the head of the river Sidon [that is, along the east side of the lake and into the wilderness], that they might come into the land of Manti and take possession of the land; for they did not suppose that the armies of Moroni would know whither they had gone." (Alma 43:22.) Naturally they would think this, for they had marched into the wilderness in a northerly direction and then circled back toward Manti in the south. (See map, "Battle with the Zoramite-led Lamanites.")

Having learned through Alma's prophetic power where the enemy had gone, Moroni left a part of his army in Jershon and marched the rest to the land of Manti. He secreted part of his army on the west of the river Sidon at Manti. (Alma 43:27, 32.) Another part he "concealed . . . on the east, and on the south of the hill Riplah." (Alma 43:31.) The hill Riplah was east of the river Sidon.

It was not long before "the Lamanites came up on the north of the hill. . . ." (Alma 43:34.) The rest of the terrible battle can be followed in Alma 43:34-54 and 44:1-20.

East Wilderness

A year or two later a lengthy and bloody war began. During this war, "Moroni caused that his armies should go forth into the east wilderness; . . . and [they] drove all the Lamanites who were in the east wilderness into their own lands, which were south of the land of Zarahemla. . . ." (Alma

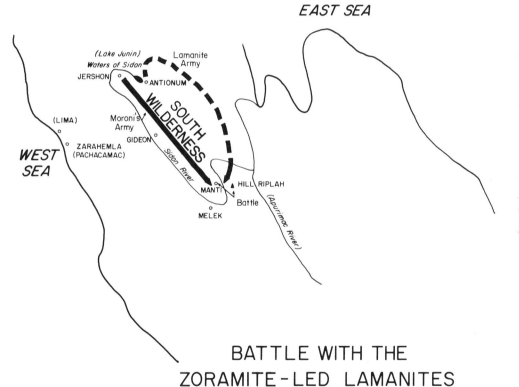

BATTLE WITH THE ZORAMITE-LED LAMANITES

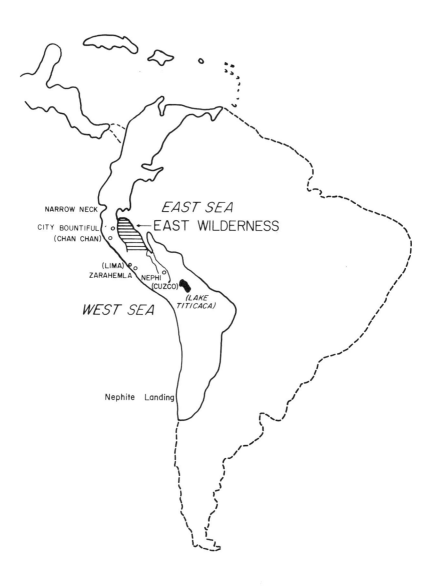

EAST WILDERNESS

50:7.) "And . . . when Moroni had driven all the Lamanites out of the east wilderness, which was north of the lands of their own possessions. . . ." (Alma 50:9), he sent some of the Nephite people into the East Wilderness to settle it. As will be seen from the map "East Wilderness," this wilderness was east of the land Bountiful and north of both Nephite and Lamanite possessions. Hence the interpretation of the words "their own possessions" in the above scripture is not important to our present purpose.

The area of the East Wilderness was, and still is, untamed wilderness. It is a part of the world's highest jungle. To travel this land today one must carry a machete. Trees and bushes alike are entangled with vines and blanketed with green moss. In some sections orchids grow in profusion. So do oranges, bananas, and other fruits, making these areas likely locations for scattered groups of unindustrious Lamanites. Through gnarled roots and dead leaves, poisonous snakes slither, jungle insects creep, and wild animals roam. Jaguars are common in this area, and chattering monkeys swing through the trees.

It is a well-known fact that white, blue-eyed, blond-haired Indians live in this area. Now known to many as the "cloud people," this white race has lived in the East Wilderness area as long as those who memorized Indian history could remember, a fact recorded by the Spanish chroniclers.[1]

At the time that Nephites moved into the East Wilderness, Moroni set about strengthening the south near the borders of the land and had his army "erect fortifications." (Alma 50:9-10.) Spanish conquistadores said that the Jauja-Huancayo valley (our valley of Gideon) ". . . was once defended on all sides by towering hills topped with fortresses."[2]

City of Moroni

It appears that simultaneous with the erection of these "fortification towers" a wide, forty-five-foot military road was being constructed. This road branched off from the main

---

[1] Gene Savoy, "Found! The Legendary 'Cloud Kingdom' of the Incas," *Argosy Magazine* (Feb. 1971), p. 55.
[2] Von Hagen, *Highway of the Sun*, p. 167.

highway at a point north of Jauja, to run northeast to what we know as the East Sea. Here "the Nephites began the foundation of a city, and they called the name of the city Moroni; and it was by the east sea; and it was on the south by the line of the possessions of the Lamanites." (Alma 50:13.) (See map, "Cities Taken by the Lamanites in the East Wilderness.")

No visible ruins of this city have come to my attention. It is recorded that it was "sunk in the depths of the sea" at the time of the crucifixion of Christ. (3 Nephi 9:4.) "Sunk in the depths of the sea" presumably means that this city, with its surrounding earth, crumbled and fell into the East Sea, where it sank to a great depth. Although the East Sea drained (this would have taken some time) and the ruins of the city might therefore have been expected to be revealed, the chances are that mud, silt, and (later) dry earth forever covered that city from view.

City of Nephihah

Nephihah, another great Nephite city, apparently arose at about the same time as the city of Moroni. This city was in the borders of the East Wilderness, inland from the East Sea, since we are told that "Amalickiah would not suffer the Lamanites to go against the city of Nephihah to battle, but kept them down by the seashore...." (Alma 51:25.) Clearly this was the East Sea seashore, since Moroni was one of the cities taken.

Amalickiah, the Nephite dissenter and king of the Lamanites, took only those cities along the East Sea shore. The scripture reads, "And thus he went on, taking possession of many cities, . . . the city of Lehi, and the city of Morianton, and the city of Omner, and the city of Gid, and the city of Mulek, all of which were on the east borders by the seashore." (Alma 51:26; see also 62:18-25.) (The mention of Nephihah in the same verse was perhaps intended to be the city of Moroni, since (1) Nephihah was by definition away from the seashore and not attacked at this time [verse 25], and (2) the Lamanites took it later [Alma 59:5-8].)

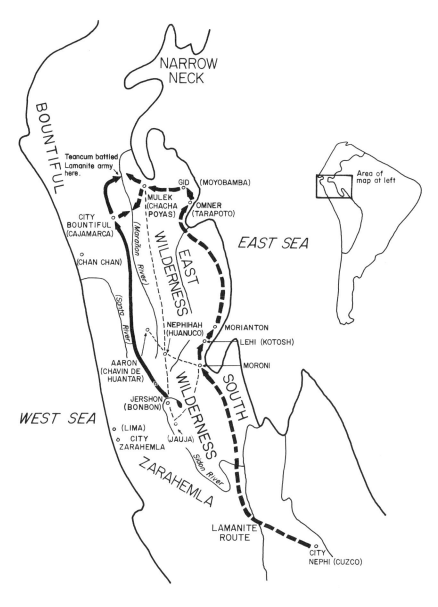

CITIES TAKEN by the LAMANITES in the EAST WILDERNESS

Most likely these cities were named in the order in which they were taken; Moroni first, it being closest to Lamanite territory, and Mulek last, it being the furthest north. From an epistle Helaman wrote to Moroni, we know that Nephihah was north of Jershon, which as we have seen was tucked in the curl of the head of Sidon. Referring to the Lamanite invaders in the southern portion of the Nephite lands, Helaman wrote: ". . . neither durst they cross the head of Sidon, over to the city of Nephihah." (Alma 56:25.)

Ruins of old Huanuco, which in all probability was Nephihah, are less than one hundred miles north of Lake Junin, the head of the Sidon.

Huanuco lay on a wide flat plain.³ Nephihah also lay on a plain large enough for Moroni and his men to "pitch their tents in the plains of Nephihah, which is near the city of Nephihah." (Alma 62:18.)

This large city of Huanuco, von Hagen tells us, was entered by way of steps and guardhouses. Four roads led from it. On the south a road moved toward Lake Junin and Jershon. On the north another road stretched to Chachapoyas near Mulek. On the east a forty-five-foot-wide military road let to Moroni (about fifty miles away). The fourth road took a northwest direction.

The City of Aaron

Alma 50:14 gives us our lead on the location of Aaron. It reads: "And they also began a foundation for a city between the city of Moroni and the city of Aaron . . . and they called the name of the city, or the land, Nephihah." Since Nephihah was "between" the cities of Moroni and Aaron, it was probably roughly equidistant from them. We have placed Moroni about fifty miles to the east of Nephihah. About fifty miles along the northwest road from Huanuco are the ruins of Chavin de Huantar. I suggest this was the city of Aaron.

Aaron was not a new city as were the cities of Nephihah and Moroni. We read of a city called Aaron about ten

---
³Von Hagen, *Highway of the Sun*, p. 186.

years earlier (Alma 8:13), when Alma first left the city of Ammonihah. He then was making for Aaron. Since Ammonihah was in the southernmost part of the land of Zarahemla near Lamanite territory, this would have meant a journey of several hundred miles to the north for Alma. It would seem that Alma intended to put as many miles as possible between him and the wicked city of Ammonihah.

Chavin de Huantar, our proposed city of Aaron, was in a deep narrow valley in the high Andes where two rivers meet. The city was mostly subterranean. There were many rooms and long corridors. The walls were lined with carefully fitted stones.[4]

The growth of Chavin de Huantar was limited. The available agricultural land could never have supported many people.[5] Perhaps this is the reason why we do not hear much of Aaron. The city must have been small and not too important.

Cities Lehi and Morianton

Ruins of numerous cities have been uncovered in our East Wilderness area, but not much has been written about them.

Lehi was built on the north by the seashore "in a particular manner. . . ." (Alma 50:15.) Could it be that the "particular manner" may have referred to "round buildings on platforms" so familiar to archaeologists who have uncovered ruins in that (East Wilderness) part of the land?

From Alma 51:26 we can conclude that Lehi was north of both Nephihah and Moroni. The most likely spot is a place called Kotosh. The Kotosh site sits at a height of about six thousand feet on the eastern slope of the Andes. A temple known as the "crossed-hands" temple was uncovered there. It was built on a twenty-five-foot-high stone-faced platform. Nothing more is known of Kotosh. Apparently the archaeological team abandoned their diggings in that area.[6] Never-

---
[4]Verrill and Verrill, *America's Ancient Civilizations,* p. 171.
[5]Alden J. Mason, *The Ancient Civilizations of Peru* (Baltimore, Maryland: Penguin Books, 1957), p. 41.
[6]Edward P. Lanning, *Peru Before the Incas* (Englewood Cliffs: Prentice-Hall, 1967), p. 92.

theless, at this point Kotosh seems the most likely choice in our search for Lehi. Lehi was close to the East Sea, Moroni, and Nephihah. When the people fled from the cities of Moroni (Alma 51:24) and of Lehi and Morianton (Alma 59:5) they ran to Nephihah.

The city Morianton was close to Lehi; so close, in fact, that a serious argument arose over the boundary lines. (Alma 50:25.) Further exploration will be needed to uncover the ruins of this city, which on the map "Mulek Retaken by Stratagem" I have tentatively shown to the north of Lehi.

Cities Omner and Gid

In the recital of Amalickiah's victories (Alma 51:26) Omner comes next in line and then Gid. These cities were probably about two hundred miles north of Lehi and Morianton. I base this conclusion on the fact that our Nephite scribe nowhere says that the people of Omner, Gid, or even Mulek fled to Nephihah, as he says of people from other cities (see above). This may have been because these cities were too far northward for this; though admittedly it could have been that the Lamanites were between them and Nephihah. More significant, perhaps, when Moroni recaptured the Lamanite-held city of Gid he did not take his prisoners to Nephihah but instead marched them to the city of Bountiful (Alma 55:26), which in our proposed geography would have been about 250 miles northwest of Nephihah.

At present it is difficult to link these two northern cities with modern discoveries. Omner may have been at Tarapoto, where the Huallaga river emptied into the East Sea. Gid could have been further north at Moyobamba (meaning "the round valley") on the Mayo river. The altitude of Moyobamba is about 2,800 feet. There are hot springs and gold placers near the city. Moyobamba was once an ancient Indian settlement under Inca influence.

While these two locations are possibilities, the cities of Omner and Gid could instead have been inland another twenty miles at Mendoza on a five-thousand-foot level. In the northernmost parts of our East Wilderness, near Mendoza, hundreds of circular white limestone buildings, sitting upon elevated platforms, have been found. Some of these buildings are two and three stories high.

The locations of the cities of Omner and Gid will remain hazy until further exploration is made in the area of the East Wilderness.

City Mulek

Mulek was the remaining city on the list and it would seem that this was near today's Chachapoyas. Apparently it was the last city to the north before reaching the land Bountiful. A forty-five-foot-wide Inca road crossed the highlands from Huanuco (Nephihah) straight to Chachapoyas, about three hundred miles distant. Chachapoyas is about 7,638 feet high and has a cold mountain climate. It is east of the Marañon river.

On this assumption as regards location, after Amalickiah had taken the city of Mulek he must have marched westward to the Marañon river. He was near that river, perhaps about to cross over it and enter into the land Bountiful, when he was met by Teancum, a great Nephite warrior, with his army.

Following the ensuing battle, Teancum camped "in the borders of the land Bountiful." Amalickiah camped "in the borders on the beach by the seashore." (Alma 51:28-32.) (See map, "Cities Taken by the Lamanites in the East Wilderness.")

Later, after Amalickiah's death, Moroni gave Teancum orders to "fortify the land Bountiful, and secure the narrow pass. . . ." (Alma 52:9.) Teancum did this, and subsequently moved south to the city Bountiful to await Moroni's arrival. (Alma 52:17.)

Moroni arrived at Bountiful and a council of war was held. (Alma 52:19.) The Lamanite leaders, who were "holed up" in Mulek, were challenged to an open battle upon the plains between Mulek and the city Bountiful. When they refused, Teancum took a small number of men and camped on the beach within sight of Mulek, and by stratagem he was able to lead the Lamanites out of the city in pursuit. At this, Moroni's previously concealed men came out of hiding and

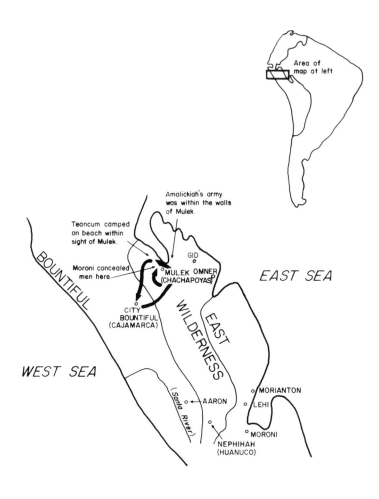

MULEK RETAKEN by STRATAGEM

took the city. Moroni left a few men at Mulek and the rest proceeded to follow the Lamanites who were pursuing Teancum toward the city Bountiful, a distance of about seventy or eighty miles. (Alma 52:18-27.)

The City Bountiful

The city Bountiful was a stronghold. (Alma 53:5.) The ruins of that city are at today's Cajamarca, a very important city even in the days of the Spanish conquest of Peru. It was at Cajamarca that Atahualpa was executed by Pizarro and his conquistadores. The city lay at an elevation of 8,500 feet. Hot sulfur springs on the outskirts of the city supplied hot water to the "bath of the Incas," a bath cut from solid rock and of about the size of a swimming pool.

The name *Cajamarca* means "town in a ravine." The city was built as a gigantic circular fortress, its buildings being constructed of cut pink granite highly polished so as to give the effect of large mirrors.[7] The buildings faced inwards from the circle embracing the city, their rear windowless walls being joined together to form a natural wall. Perhaps this eliminated the need for a great wall around the city; and it could have had something to do with Moroni's having a ditch dug around the city Bountiful, a breastwork of timbers built upon the inner bank of the ditch, and earth thrown out of the ditch against the timbers. (Alma 53:3-4.) Over the centuries a fortification of this type (timber and earth) would have decayed and disappeared.

The Land (County) Bountiful

The county land of Bountiful stretched northward approximately from Paramonga to Tumbes and the narrow neck of land; and it moved eastward from the Pacific Ocean to the Marañon river. Notice that this land, like the county land of Zarahemla, was roughly oblong in shape.

The coastal lands of this area today are desert except for an occasional green section irrigated by a stream jetting down out of the Andes toward the Pacific. In the inter-Andean

---

[7]Verrill and Verrill, *America's Ancient Civilizations*, p. 166.

BOUNTIFUL

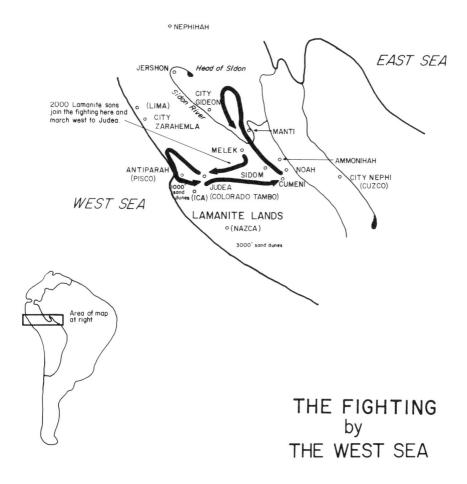

THE FIGHTING
by
THE WEST SEA

valleys of this land, green corn, squash, avocados and other kinds of food grow in profusion. On the hills of these valleys abundant grass grows for grazing llama and alpaca herds. The harvest of this land, formerly known as the land Bountiful, is indeed bountiful.

Fighting on the West Sea

Fighting erupted on the south and on the west of the land of Zarahemla. On the south, in the high Andes, the Lamanites seized the city of Manti, along with a few other mountain lands. The fighting then spread westerly along the southern border to as far as the West Sea. The Nephite army was close to destruction in that quarter of the land when the people of Ammon sent two thousand of their sons to join the fighting. (Alma 53:22; 56:9-15.)

Looking back to the map, "King's Lands," we see that the Lamanites already had some possessions in the borders of Zarahemla by the seashore. What is now Nazca was one of those lands. Ica was another. Ica was about forty miles inland from the sea and was northward from Nazca. The fighting on the West Sea took place to the north of the Lamanite-held land of Ica. Pisco is north of Ica and no doubt was the Nephite city Antiparah. East of Ica was Colorado (colorful) Tambo. This undoubtedly would have been Judea.

In joining the army of Antipus, Helaman and his two thousand stripling soldiers apparently marched from Melek (Alma 35:13) westward to Judea (Alma 56:15). The course of the fighting in that area, as set out in Helaman's epistle to Moroni (Alma 56-58) can be followed by referring to the map "The Fighting by the West Sea."

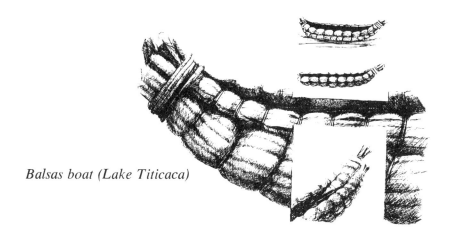

Balsas boat (Lake Titicaca)

CHAPTER 10

The Land Changed

Shortly after General Moroni's death "a large company of men, even to the amount of five thousand and four hundred men, with their wives and their children, departed out of the land of Zarahemla [55 B.C.] into the land which was northward." (Alma 63:4.)

Another group of people left Zarahemla for the land northward several years later (46 B.C.). These people, many of whom were of the people of Ammon, or Lamanites (Helaman 3:12), traveled to at least as far as Ecuador. (Helaman 3:3-5.) These northward-migrating people became expert in the working of cement,[1] their land being almost devoid of timber. (Helaman 3:6-7.) It is noted that traces of what used to be stone cities are today found throughout Ecuador.

Shipping and the building of ships became the basis of communication between the land northward and the land southward. (Alma 63:10; Helaman 3:10, 14.) In fact, it appears that ships were of irreplaceable service when the

---

[1]The word *cement* comes from the Latin verb "to cut" and originally had reference to stonecutting.

people began "to cover the face of the whole earth, from the sea south to the sea north, from the sea west to the sea east" (Helaman 3:8); or, in other words, when the Nephite Island became inhabited from the sea south of that island to the Caribbean Sea, and from the Pacific Ocean on the west to the Amazon Sea on the east.

Shipping and the building of ships (Helaman 3:14) not only indicate short, close-to-shore voyages,[2] but long seaward voyages. Because the records of these migrating people were not included in the records kept by the Nephites who remained in the land southward (Helaman 3:14-16), in order to follow their movements it is necessary to rely upon archaeological discoveries. It will be apparent, after reading the next three sections ("The Inscribed Stone," "Nephite Altar," and "Zelph, the White Lamanite"), that some of the above-mentioned sailors moved by ship onto the North American continent by way of the great North American waterway. That waterway was navigable for a distance of 2,500 miles. Today it is called the Mississippi river. By following this river some of the descendants of the South American peoples would have found new land in that part of the North American continent.

The Inscribed Stone

Some evidences of these early migrating people have been found in land sections not far removed from the Mississippi. An example is the inscribed stone found in a burial mound at Bat Creek, Tennessee, east of the Mississippi. The stone was under one of nine skeletons in the mound. Cyrus H. Gordon, Professor of Mediterranean Studies at Brandeis University, said that the writing style on the stone was like that

---

[2]Skills of the stonecutter are found on the Caribbean side of the Santa Marta mountains, as if they had come in from the sea.

Had the "Darien Gap" (eastern Panama) been above water as it is today (blocking free sailing into the Caribbean from the Pacific) there would have been two other possible routes whereby one might reach the Caribbean. The first route would have been over exceedingly difficult terrain, from Quito, Ecuador, to Pasto, Colombia, to the Cauca river depression which lies between Colombia's Central and Western Cordilleras, and on to the Caribbean. A second route would have been by sea from Ecuador to the mouth of the Patia river. By following this river inland it is possible to move up into the Cauca depression and on to the Caribbean.

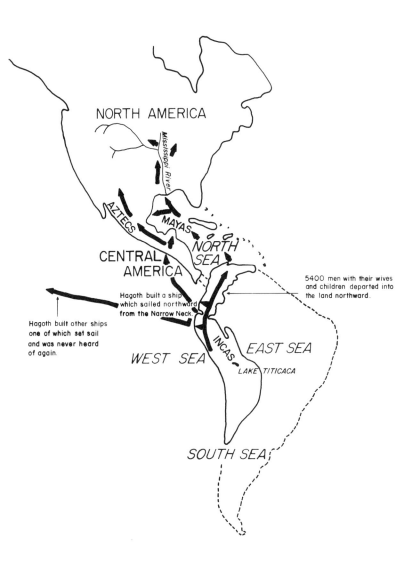

MIGRATION of the PEOPLE

of ancient Canaan, the Israelites' "promised land." The fifth letter, he said, corresponded to the style of writing found on ancient Hebrew coins.[3] Note that Nephi said: ". . . I make a record in the language of my father, which consists of the learning of the Jews and the language of the Egyptians."[4] (1 Nephi 1:2.) The inscribed stone found in Tennessee is strong evidence of the origin of the people who buried it.

Nephite Altar or Tower

Another important find, known only to members of The Church of Jesus Christ of Latter-day Saints, was made further up the Mississippi and west into Davis County, Missouri. Here Joseph Smith discovered the remains of an old Nephite altar or tower. The altar was about sixteen feet long and nine or ten feet wide. Its height was about two and one-half feet on each end, gradually rising to about four or five feet in the center.[5]

Zelph, the White Lamanite

Wars and contentions plagued the inhabitants who had moved onto the North American continent. The remains of Zelph, the white Lamanite, were found by the members of Zion's Camp on the trek from Ohio to Missouri. Zelph's skeleton was found about one foot beneath the earth. Between his ribs was the arrow which caused his death. Joseph Smith's account of this discovery is as follows:

"I discovered that the person whose skeleton we had seen was a white Lamanite, a large, thick-set man, and a man of God. His name was Zelph. He was a warrior and chieftain under the great prophet Onandagus, who was known from the eastern sea to the Rocky mountains. The curse was taken from Zelph, or, at least, in part — one of his thigh bones was broken by a stone flung from a sling, while in battle, years

---

[3]Associated Press news item, *San Francisco Chronicle*, October 19, 1970.

[4]For information on the influence of the Egyptian language and culture on the eastern Mediterranean countries, see Hugh Nibley's book *Lehi in the Desert* pages 10 and 11 (published by Bookcraft, 1952).

[5]William E. Berrett, *Readings in L.D.S. Church History*, vol. I (Salt Lake City, Utah: Deseret Book Company, 1953), p. 118.

before his death. He was killed in battle by the arrow found among his ribs, during a great struggle with the Lamanites."[6]

Because the story of Zelph is worded differently in the current edition of the *Documentary History of the Church,* our attention is turned to Fletcher B. Hammond's book *Geography of the Book of Mormon* (Bookcraft, 1960, pp. 102-103), wherein he refers to careful examination of a microfilm copy of the original entry in the Prophet's journal, which he says indicates that the 1904 edition of the *Documentary History of the Church* correctly reproduces the words of that entry, whereas the current edition does not. The words, "the hill Cumorah" and "the last great struggle of the Lamanites and the Nephites," in the current edition, are not in the original, he says. Thus Zelph was killed during "a" great struggle with the Lamanites. This does not say that he was killed during the final struggle. Notice too that, in the Prophet's words, Onandagus was known from the eastern sea to the Rocky mountains, not from the East Sea to the West Sea.

Aztecs

A. Hyatt and Ruth Verrill make this comment: ". . . We believe, as do several well-known archaeologists [who have studied Indian cultures of both Central and South America], that the ancestors of the ancient Mexicans came from northern Peru, in the vicinity of . . . Ancash and Junin."[7]

Traditions say that the original home of the ancient Mexicans was in some unknown area called Aztlan or "Place of the Reeds."[8] That home could have been Lake Titicaca, in which case the ancient Mexicans or Aztec people could have been a remnant of the people who were called Anti-Nephi-Lehies, later the people of Ammon. (See chapter 8, heading "Anti-Nephi-Lehies.")

Totora or balsas reeds, not to be confused with the balsa tree mentioned below, have always grown in profusion in the

---

[6]*Documentary History of the Church,* Vol. II, 1904 edition, pp. 79-80, as quoted in *U.A.S. Newsletter,* January 30, 1963.
[7]Verrill and Verrill, *America's Ancient Civilizations,* p. 92.
[8]Verrill and Verrill, *America's Ancient Civilizations,* p. 52.

shallow fringes of Lake Titicaca. For centuries, people who have lived near this lake have used the balsas reeds for mats and boats. Today at Titicaca, a group of lake people live on artificial islands made of thickly matted totora or balsas reeds. Huts made of the same reeds are built on top of these islands. Balsas boats are used to move about the lake. Air in the reeds keeps the islands and boats afloat for only six months; therefore, constant building and repairing is required.

When the people called Anti-Nephi-Lehies moved from the Titicaca basin they came northward to a land called Jershon on the west shores of Lake Junin. Some of these people were among those who migrated into the land northward B.C., and who built ships (Helaman 3:3, 4, 12, 14.)

The people of Ammon or Anti-Nephi-Lehi could have found and settled Mexico, their descendants later building their capital on the marshy shores of a lake in a situation reminiscent of their ancestral homes near Lake Titicaca and Lake Junin.

Hagoth Builds a Ship

About the same time the first recorded northward migration was taking place (55 B.C.), a man named Hagoth was building a ship "on the borders of the land Bountiful, by the land Desolation. . . ." (Alma 63:5.) The light and buoyant wood of the balsa tree may well have been used in the construction of his ship. This tree grows in northern South America in the vicinity of today's Tumbes.

When Hagoth's ship was completed, he "launched it forth into the west sea, by the narrow neck. . . ." (Alma 63:5.) Most likely Hagoth's ship sailed from Tumbes northward (Alma 63:6) to as far as Guatemala. From that point the people probably fanned out upon the face of the land, to build great cities in Guatemala, Yucatan, parts of Mexico, and western Panama. (The "Darien Gap," comprising eastern Panama, beginning thirty-five miles east of Panama city and stretching 150 air miles to the Colombian border, appears to be without signs of civilized tribes. See chapter 2, heading "The Narrow Neck.")

Hagoth built more than one ship. The first returned, took on other passengers, and set sail; but it was never heard of again. The record tells of another ship which sailed forth, but what happened to it is not known. (Alma 63:8.) It is supposed that these people drifted to the islands of the Pacific.

Matthew Cowley, the apostle, tells of the time he spent as a missionary among the Maori people. He said: "I used to ask the oldtimers out there, 'Where did you come from?' They would say (in Maori), 'We come from the place where the sweet potato grows wild, where it is not planted, does not have to be cultivated!' "[9] Sweet potatoes, we are told, "were grown by the Incas of South America hundreds of years ago."[10] South America seems to be the native home of the sweet potato.

Great Wall

Eventually the Lamanites succeeded in taking possession of the land and city of Zarahemla, as well as all the surrounding lands and cities as far north as "the land which was near the land Bountiful." (Helaman 4:5.) "And the Nephites and the armies of Moronihah were driven even into the land of Bountiful; and there they did fortify against the Lamanites, from the west sea, even unto the east; it being a day's journey for a Nephite [runner], on the line which they had fortified and stationed their armies to defend their north country." (Helaman 4:6-7.)

As stated earlier, a day's journey was about fifty miles for a Nephite. Therefore the Nephite fortifications would have run from the West Sea (Pacific Ocean) inland about forty or fifty miles.

The remains of a great wall run from the Pacific Ocean inland along the Santa river for about forty miles. The Santa river and the ruins of the great rough-stone wall are located in what we are calling the land of Bountiful. The wall itself runs mainly along the north of the river, crossing sometimes

---

[9]Matthew Cowley, *Matthew Cowley Speaks* (Salt Lake City, Utah: Deseret Book Company, 1954), p. 114.
[10]William Benton (publisher), "Sweet Potato," *Encyclopaedia Britannica Jr.,* vol. 13, 1960, p. 548.

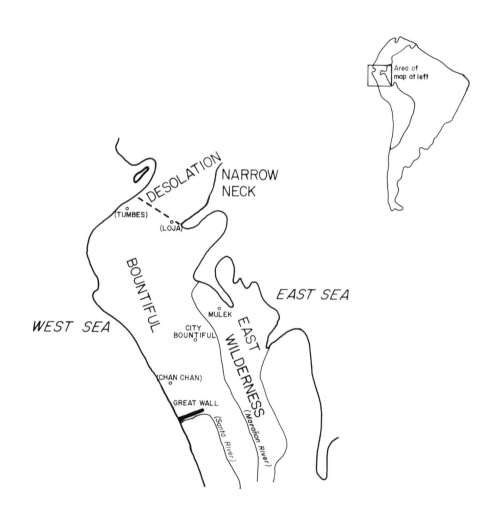

THE GREAT WALL

to the south bank as dictated by land contour and the river's course. Forty or fifty man-made fortresses run along the length of the wall, all on top of the highest hills. None are connected to the wall. Evidently some of the fortresses were round, some square, others rectangular. Each fortress enclosed an area of about two hundred by three hundred feet.[11]

Explorer Gene Savoy found that the wall was ten feet high in some places and as thick as fifteen feet.[12] This great Peruvian wall and its fortresses along the Santa river fit very well the description of the fortifications in the land of Bountiful spoken of in Helaman chapter 4.

Whole Face of the Land Changed

". . . For behold, the whole face of the land was changed, because of the tempest and the whirlwinds and the thunderings and the lightnings, and the exceeding great quaking of the whole earth." (3 Nephi 8:12.)

The language of this scripture would indicate that catastrophic changes in the "face of the land" took place along the entire length of the Nephite Island from the Caribbean to the tip of Chile. Geological evidences such as the heaving upward of lower Chile from the ocean's bottom, the rising of Tiahuanaco to about 3,400 feet above its previous level, and the possible rising of the 150-mile "Darien Gap" at Panama show this to be true. Apparently all the geological changes took place within the space of three hours. (3 Nephi 8:19.)

Volcanic eruptions along the so-called "fire-lane," which stretches along the entire length of the Andes mountains, could easily have been the means the Lord used to effect these changes. Chain-reaction volcanic activity is not an uncommon thing along the fire-lane. Charles Darwin tells of seeing the volcano Osorno erupt while he stood on the deck of the *Beagle*. The erupting volcano was about forty miles inland.

---

[11]Philip Ainsworth Means, "The Incas, Empire Builders of the Andes," *Indians of the Americas* (Washington, D.C.; National Geographic Society, 1957), pp. 284-285; also Victor W. von Hagen, *The Desert Kingdoms of Peru* (Conn.: New York Graphic Society, Ltd., 1965), p. 124.

[12]Victor Wolfgang von Hagen, *The Desert Kingdoms of Peru* (Greenwich, Connecticut: New York Graphic Society, Ltd., 1965), p. 124.

Darwin was surprised to hear afterwards that the Aconcagua, another volcano located about 480 miles northward of Osorno, had also erupted. He was even more surprised when he heard that the volcano Coseguina, about 2,700 miles north of the volcano Aconcagua, had erupted, causing a great earthquake which was felt within a thousand-mile radius. The Coseguina erupted within six hours of the others.[13] According to his report, volcanic activity can, and sometimes does, take place almost simultaneously along this fire belt.

Volcanic action could have given rise not only to the earthquakes and avalanches (3 Nephi 9:5) but also to the tempests, including hail, strong winds, and rain (3 Nephi 8:12), lightning, thunder, whirlwinds and tornadoes (3 Nephi 8:12, 16), and fire and hot lava (3 Nephi 9:11). Frank W. Lane said that weather in the immediate area of a volcano is largely created by the effects of the eruption. "In all violent eruptions there are thunderstorms with brilliant lightning, hail, and heavy rains."[14] "The great heat in some eruptions also caused tornadoes."[15] For example: "During the great eruption of Tambora [Indonesia] in April 1815, the most violent tornadoes formed. They snatched up men, horses, cattle, and anything movable. The largest trees were torn out of the ground by the roots and whirled into the air."[16] This too is consistent with the Book of Mormon account, wherein we read: "And there were some who were carried away in the whirlwind; and whither they went no man knoweth. . . ." (3 Nephi 8:16.)

The upheavals around Zarahemla and Bountiful would have been heavy, but in the land northward they must have been of tremendous magnitude. The records says, "there was a more great and terrible destruction in the land northward. . . ." (3 Nephi 8:12.) There are about twenty-two very high peaks in Ecuador. Most of them are cones. Mt. Chimborazo could have erupted, along with several others in that area,

---
[13]Darwin, *Beagle,* pp. 278-279.
[14]Frank W. Lane, *The Elements Rage* (Philadelphia: Chilton Book Company, 1965), pp. 253-254. Copyright © 1965 by the author. Used with permission.
[15]Lane, *The Elements Rage,* p. 254.
[16]Lane, *The Elements Rage,* p. 254.

leaving the land scorched and burned, trees uprooted, some cities flattened and some buried beneath tons of lava and volcanic ash.

As we saw in chapter 1, Charles Darwin claimed that the Andes, along the lower half of Chile, had been raised in a very recent period, geologically speaking. R. T. Chamberlin tells us that when the Andes rose in South America, "hundreds, if not thousands, of cubic miles of the body of the earth almost instantaneously heaved upward [producing] a violent earthquake which spread . . . throughout the entire globe."[17]

After three hours the quaking and tempests stopped. (3 Nephi 8:19.) Thick darkness settled over the land, presumably in the form of ash and dust clouds; a darkness which lasted three days. (3 Nephi 8:23.) Following the eruption of Tambora, Indonesia (April 1815), "a vast dust cloud turned day into night for hundreds of miles around the volcano, darkness . . . lasted for three days. . . ."[18] The same thing was true at Madura 310 miles away.

While there was tremendous destruction, the sites of some cities remained unchanged. For instance, Zarahemla burned but was later rebuilt. Other cities and lands were also restored. (4 Nephi 7-8.) Apparently the Sidon river still flowed much as it had before the catastrophe. (Mormon 1:10.)

Where Christ Appeared

Some time after the great destruction, Christ appeared to a group of people who were gathered in the land Bountiful near the temple. (3 Nephi 10:18; 11:1.) The land Bountiful in this instance could have been and probably was the county land rather than the city land of Bountiful. (See chapter 9.) The people were conversing about the great changes which had taken place in the different parts of the land. The thought occurs that the occasion for this gathering may have been a conference of the Church, for there were about 2,500 people

---
[17]Velikovsky, *Earth in Upheaval*, p. 151.
[18]Lane, *The Elements Rage*, p. 251.

there. (3 Nephi 17:25.) Nephi the prophet was among them. (3 Nephi 11:18.)

After the Lord Jesus Christ had visited the land and taught the people, there was peace and righteousness for about two hundred years. Then wickedness gradually began to develop, until by the time Mormon took up the story (around A.D. 320) both Nephites and Lamanites "had become exceeding wicked. . . ." (4 Nephi 45.) This lengthy period from A.D. 34 to 320 is covered briefly in four Book of Mormon pages which apparently contain no geographical information.

Inca nobleman (Peru)

CHAPTER 11
Mormon, Moroni and Cumorah

It appears that when Mormon was very young (Mormon 1:2) he lived in the land northward, probably Ecuador. There are two reasons for believing this: (1) The prophet Ammaron hid the Nephite records in the hill Shim, which was in the land northward (Mormon 1:2-3; Ether 9:3; see chapter 3, heading "Hill Shim."); he then revealed their hiding-place to Mormon. (2) The following year, according to Mormon: "I, being eleven years old, was carried by my father into the land southward. . . ." (Mormon 1:6.)

After Mormon arrived in the land southward, about A.D. 322, ". . . war began to be among them in the borders of Zarahemla, by the waters of Sidon." (Mormon 1:10.) This time the Nephites beat back the enemy attack, but five years later (about A.D. 327) the Lamanites came with such force that the Nephites ". . . began to retreat towards the north countries." (Mormon 2:3.) That is, they fled northward into the county land of Bountiful. The Lamanites continued their attacks until they had driven the Nephites into the land northward. (Mormon 2:15-17.) For Mormon, this ended a twenty-three-year stay in the land southward.

In the three hundred and fiftieth year a treaty was made with the Lamanites. (Mormon 2:28-29.) All the land north of the narrow pass, or all the land northward (Ecuador and Colombia and beyond) was given to the Nephites. Even so, there may have been descendants of Lamanites — descendants of the people of Ammon — who shared this land with the Nephites, since four hundred years previously "many" of the people of Ammon had moved into the land northward (Helaman 3:12), and perhaps some of them survived the great destruction at the time of the crucifixion of Christ. The aggressive Lamanites and robbers, who had driven the Nephites into the land northward, were given all the land southward (Mormon 2:29), that is, everything south of the Gulf of Guayaquil. After this the enemy did not make war again on the Nephites for another ten years. (Mormon 3:1.)

When the Lamanite king once again made war, Mormon fortified the county land Desolation "by the narrow pass which led into the land southward." (Mormon 3:5.) With the narrow pass blocked, the Lamanites came "down to the city Desolation to battle. . . ." (Mormon 3:7.) Assuming that the Oro pass, which is north of Loja, was the same pass spoken of in the Book of Mormon, we know that the Lamanites, not being able to move further northward, turned westward from Loja down to the coast. (See chapter 2.) The city Desolation was by the seashore. The Nephites were victorious, as they were also when the enemy returned the following year. Many Lamanites were killed and "their dead were cast into the sea." (Mormon 3:8.)

After the Nephites had made an unsuccessful venture into Lamanite territory the Lamanites came again. This time they took possession of the city Desolation (Mormon 4:2-13) and also the city Teancum, which was near the city Desolation. (Mormon 4:14.) Once more, in about A.D. 367, the Nephites managed to retake their lands, but eight years later the enemy returned in overpowering numbers and drove and slaughtered the Nephites. (Mormon 4:15-18.) Mormon knew that it was

Mormon, Moroni and Cumorah 155

impossible to save the land, so he went "to the hill Shim [cerro Hermoso — see chapter 3, heading "Hill Shim"], and did take up all the records which Ammaron had hid. . . ."[1] (Mormon 4:23.) Within a few more years the Nephites had been pushed northward to their final battleground, the Cumorah area.

Mormon recognized that the Nephites were about to engage in their last and fatal struggle with the Lamanites. The sacred records must not be allowed to fall into enemy hands. He wrote: "I . . . hid up in the hill Cumorah all the records . . . save it were these few plates which I gave unto my son Moroni." (Mormon 6:6.)

Some time before the final battle, Mormon wrote a letter to his son Moroni wherein he said: "I trust that I may see thee soon; for I have sacred records that I would deliver up unto thee." (Moroni 9:24.) "These few plates" (Mormon's abridged record, plus some others) appear to be the only records given over to Moroni's charge (Mormon 6:6), indicating that the brass plates and the unabridged Nephite plates had already been hidden in the hill Cumorah and sealed up unto God. On this basis the plates which Mormon gave to his son Moroni would have included Mormon's abridgment of the Nephite records and the small plates of Nephi. Moroni also had the twenty-four Jaredite gold plates in his possession at some point, since he finished abridging them toward the end of his life. (Moroni 1:1.)

Mormon knew that an abridgment of the Jaredite records would be made, as is indicated by his comment in the book of Mosiah: "And this account [Jaredite account] shall be written hereafter; for behold, it is expedient that all people should know the things which are written in this account." (Mosiah 28:19.) No new plates were made by Moroni. He said: "Ore I have none . . . I am alone." (Mormon 8:5.) This being the case, it is obvious that "these few plates" which Mormon gave to his son Moroni included a few extra plates

---

[1]The plates were removed from the hill Shim approximately ten years before the final battle — about A.D. 375.

upon which Moroni was to write the abridged history of the Jaredite people.[2]

The possibility that Moroni stayed near the hill Cumorah after the final battle is remote. At least 230,000 Nephites, with their wives and children, were slain at Cumorah and their bodies ". . . lay upon the face of the earth . . . to molder upon the land, and to crumble and to return to their mother earth." (Mormon 6:15.) The stench of the dead, if nothing else, would have driven Moroni from Cumorah. The site of the wicked city Ammonihah had been left desolate for many years for that very reason.[3] (Alma 16:11.) Polluted land and water would also have caused Moroni to leave. Typhus and *verruga*, a deadly Andean disease spread by sandflies, would have become a threat to anyone remaining in that area.

Moroni would not have moved southward. He wrote, ". . . behold, the Nephites who had escaped into the country southward were hunted by the Lamanites, until they were all destroyed" (Mormon 8:2); nor would he have moved into the Amazon jungle, it being a difficult place for a man alone. Logically Moroni would have moved northward into Colombia, but of this we cannot be sure. Mormon 8:3 does not say that he remained in Cumorah, nor does it say that he moved away, only that he was left alone "to write the sad tale." Verse 4 likewise does not say that he remained in Cumorah. It says only that after he had written his account he would hide the records in the earth. From Ether 1:1 we know that when Moroni commenced his abridgment of the Jaredite records, he was in the land northward. This could have been in Ecuador or Colombia. Mormon 8:8 exclaims: "The Lamanites are at war one with another." This war may

---

[2]After the abridgment of the Jaredite records was completed, enough room remained for Moroni to write those things which are contained in the book of Moroni, plus the title page. Joseph Smith said of the title page: "I wish to mention here that the title-page of the Book of Mormon is a literal translation, taken from the very last leaf, on the left hand side of the collection or book of plates, which contained the record which has been translated. . . ." (Joseph Smith, *History of the Church,* vol. 1, p. 71.)

[3]In January 1962 a Peruvian avalanche buried 3,500 people. Later, though the bodies were covered with earth, "the valley wore a sickly-sweet stench." (Bart McDowell, "Avalanche!" *National Geographic Magazine,* June 1962, p. 880.)

have been among recent Lamanite arrivals from the south and possibly also permanent Lamanite residents of the land northward — descendants of the people of Ammon. Such wars may have taken place in Ecuador or Colombia or both.

During the fifteen or more years following the final battle (Mormon 8:6; Moroni 1:3), it is not clear where Moroni traveled. He said: "I wander whithersoever I can for the safety of mine own life."[4] (Moroni 1:3.)

We cannot know how a lone man, of himself, could have made the long trek from South America to North America to bury the plates in a hill in New York State. We can readily believe that the all-powerful God could have given him the wisdom, strength and food to survive, thereby making such a long journey both possible and bearable. Clearly, all things are possible with God (Alma 7:8), and the way was opened for Moroni to place the Book of Mormon record in the North American hill where many centuries later it would be brought forth to the world by the great prophet and seer of the last dispensation, Joseph Smith.

---

[4] A total of about thirty-six years elapsed from the final battle at Cumorah until the last inscription was made by Moroni on the abridged plates.

Bibliography

Abercrombie, Thomas J. "Behind the Veil of Troubled Yemen." *The National Geographic Magazine* (March 1964).
Arnov, Boris Jr. *Secrets of Inland Waters.* Boston: Little, Brown and Company, 1965.
Beals, Carleton. *Nomads and Empire Builders.* Philadelphia: Chilton Book Company, 1961.
Benton, William (Publisher). "Amazon River, South America." *Britannica Junior,* Vol. 2, 1960.
———. "South America." *Britannica Junior,* Vol. 13, 1960.
———. "Sweet Potato." *Britannica Junior,* Vol. 13, 1960.
Berrett, William E. *Readings in L.D.S. Church History,* Vol. 1. Salt Lake City, Utah: Deseret Book Company, 1953.
Bingham, Hiram. *Lost City of the Incas.* New York: Hawthorn Books, Inc., 1948.
Blanchard, Dean Hobbs. *Ecuador, Crown Jewel of the Andes.* New York: Vantage Press, 1962.
Cowley, Matthew. *Matthew Cowley Speaks.* Salt Lake City, Utah: Deseret Book Company, 1954.
Darwin, Charles. *The Voyage of the Beagle.* London: J. M. Dent and Sons, 1906.
Flornoy, Bertrand. *World of the Incas.* New York: Vanguard Press, Inc., 1965.
Garcilaso de la Vega. *The Incas,* 1539-1616, translated by Maria Jolas. New York: Grossman Publishers, 1961.
Glueck, Nelson. *Rivers in the Desert.* New York: Farrar, Straus and Giroux, Inc., 1959.
Gordon, Cyrus H. "Jews May Have Beat Columbus." *Associated Press, San Francisco Chronicle,* October 19, 1970.

———. *Before Columbus.* New York: Crown Publications, Inc., 1971.

Gresswell, R. Kay, and Huxley, Anthony, (eds.) "Amazon." *Standard Encyclopedia of the World's Rivers and Lakes.* New York: G. P. Putnam's Sons, 1965.

Hammond, Fletcher B. *Geography of the Book of Mormon.* Salt Lake City, Utah: Bookcraft, Inc., 1960.

Hanson, Earl Parker, and Butland, Gilbert James. "Paraguay." *Encyclopaedia Britannica,* Vol. 17, 1973.

Hapgood, Charles H. *The Path of the Pole.* Philadelphia: Chilton Book Company, 1970.

Hastings, James (ed.) *Dictionary of the Bible.* New York: Charles Scribner's Sons, 1952.

Hewett, Edgar L. *Ancient Andean Life.* New York: The Bobbs-Merrill Company, Inc., 1936.

Lamoureux, Andrew Jackson. "Ecuador." *Encyclopaedia Britannica,* 11th edition, 1922, Vol. 8.

Lane, Frank W. *The Elements Rage.* Philadelphia: Chilton Book Company, 1965.

Lanning, Edward P. *Peru Before the Incas.* New Jersey: Prentice-Hall, Inc., 1967.

Larson, Robert. "Was America the Wonderful Land of Fusang?" *American Heritage.* New York: American Heritage Publishing Co., April 1966.

Mason, J. Alden. *The Ancient Civilizations of Peru.* Baltimore, Md.: Penguin Books, 1957.

McDowell, Bart. "Avalanche!" *National Geographic Magazine,* June 1962.

McIntyre, Loren. "Ecuador — Low and Lofty Land Astride the Equator." *National Geographic Magazine,* February 1968.

Means, Philip Ainsworth. *Ancient Civilizations of the Andes.* New York: Charles Scribner's Sons, 1931.

———. "The Incas, Empire Builders of the Andes." *Indians of the Americas.* Washington D.C.: National Geographic Society, 1957.

Merriam-Webster, A. *Webster's New Geographical Dictionary.* Springfield, Mass.: G. and C. Merriam Co., 1972.

Nibley, Hugh. *Lehi in the Desert.* Salt Lake City, Utah: Bookcraft, Inc., 1952.

Niles, Blair. *Peruvian Pageant.* New York: The Bobbs-Merrill Company, Inc., 1937.

Phillips, Wendell. *Qataban and Sheba.* New York: Collins-Knowlton-Wing, Inc., 1955.

Pratt, Orson. "America a Choice Land — its Aborigines," *Journal of Discourses.* London, England: Albert Carrington, 1869, Vol. 12.

Price, Willard. *The Amazing Amazon.* New York: The John Day Co., Inc., 1952.

Savoy, Gene. "Found! The Legendary 'Cloud Kingdom' of the Incas." *Argosy Magazine,* February 1971.

Schmid, Peter. *Beggars on Golden Stools,* translated by Mervyn Savill. New York: Frederick A. Praeger, Inc., 1956.

Seltzer, Leon E. (ed.) *The Columbia Lippincott Gazetteer of the World.* New York: Columbia University Press, 1962.

Smith, Joseph. *History of The Church of Jesus Christ of Latter-day Saints,* Vol. II. Salt Lake City, Utah: Deseret News, 1948.

Steward, Julian H. (ed.) "The Andean Civilizations." *Handbook of South American Indians,* Vol. 2.

Velikovsky, Immanuel. *Earth in Upheaval.* New York: Doubleday and Company, 1955.

Verrill, A. Hyatt. *Old Civilizations of the New World.* Indianapolis: The Bobbs-Merrill Company, Inc., 1929.

Verrill, A. Hyatt, and Verrill, Ruth. *America's Ancient Civilizations.* New York: G. P. Putnam's Sons, 1953.

Von Hagen, Victor Wolfgang. *Ecuador and the Galapagos Islands.* Oklahoma: The University of Oklahoma Press, 1949.

———. *Highway of the Sun.* New York: Duell, Sloan and Pearce, Inc. in association with Little, Brown and Company, 1955.

———. *South America Called Them.* New York: Alfred A. Knopf, Inc., 1945.

———. *The Desert Kingdoms of Peru.* Connecticut: New York Graphic Society, Ltd., 1965.

Webb, Kempton E. "Amazon River." *Encyclopedia Americana,* Vol. I, 1971.

White, Orland Emile. "Amazon." *Encyclopaedia Britannica,* Vol. I, 1971.

Ybarra, T. R. *Lands of the Andes.* New York: Coward-McCann, 1947.

Index

-A-

Aaron, city of, 132-133
Abinadi, 85, 90
Ablom, by the seashore, 45-46
Aconcagua, eruption of volcano, 150
Agosh, plains of, 52-53
Akish, wilderness of, 50-52
Alma the older, baptisms in Mormon, 90
  escape of people of, 96-98
Altar or tower, Nephite, found in Missouri, 144
Alvarado, Pedro de, route to Quito, 41
Amalickiah, 130
Amazing Amazon, The, by Willard Price, 13
Amazon basin, formerly fresh-water sea, 10-13
  low level of, 12
Amazon river, delta of, 19
  depth of, 12
  flows through break, 18
  once a sea, 13-16
  pass from Quito to, 50
Amazon sea, evidence for, 10-13
Ambato, Ecuador, 41, 50
  early pottery discovery near, 37
Ambi river, 55
America's Ancient Civilizations, by A. Hyatt and Ruth Verrill, 38
Amlici, makes war with Nephites, 103-106
Ammaron, 153
  words to Mormon, 43
Ammon (sent from Zarahemla), in Limhi's kingdom, 93-96
Ammon (son of Mosiah), in land of Ishmael, 115-117
Ammonihah, city of, 107
Amnihu, hill, 103
Amulon, city of, 90
  Lamanites find city of, 96

Anaquito plains, identified with plains of Heshlon, 50
Andes mountains, 10, 14, 31
  Chile, raised in recent period, 151
Ani-Anti, village of, 120
Anti-Nephi-Lehies, explanation of name, 118-119
  move to Zarahemla, 121-123
Antionum, land of, 125
  near seashore, 4
Antipus, 140
Antisuyu road, 76, 82, 84, 87
Antum, 43
Apurimac river, 73, 91
  sudden rise during storm, 98
Arequipa, Peru, Middoni probably near today's, 120
  on Inca road, 68
Argentina, formerly inundated, 10-16
  raising of land in, 14
Asillo, identified with Jerusalem, 120
Atlantic ocean, formerly reached Andes, 15
Avalanches, 150
Aztecs, 38
  possible origin in northern Peru, 145-146

-B-

Ball, carried by Nephi, 65
Balsas reeds, lakes Titicaca and Junin, 145-146
Bat Creek, Tennessee, inscribed stone found at, 142-144
Before Columbus, by Cyrus H. Gordon, 16-18
Benjamin, speaks outside of temple, 100
Bingham, Hyrum, *Lost City of the Incas,* 85
Bonbon, Peru, identified with Jershon, 123

164   Index

Bondage, Nephites in, 88, 93
Bountiful, city of, 137
Bountiful, land of, 3, 27
   bordered on Desolation, 30
   fortifications, 136, 147-148
   in relation to Desolation, 1
   part of land southward, 3
   size and shape, 137-140
Brazil, highlands, 18
Buenos Aires, 15
Butland, Gilbert James, on ancient South American sea, 15

-C-

Cajamarca, Peru, 31
   identified with Bountiful, 137
Calderon plains, Ecuador, identified with plains of Heshlon, 50
"Came over," significance of term, 38
Canaanites, in Brazil, stone left by, 16-18
Cañar, Ecuador, early pottery discovered near, 37
Caráques, Ecuador, landing-place of Indian forbears, 34
   climatic conditions, 34-35
Catari, Inca quipu-keeper, 33-34
Cayambe, Ecuador, 44
   identified with valley of Shurr, 54
Cement, expert work in, 141
Chachapoyas, Peru, 132
   identified with Mulek, 135
Chanapata, Peru, identified with Shemlon, 81
Chavin de Huantar, Peru, identified with Aaron, 133
Chile, has biggest open-pit copper mine, 64
   southern half of, formerly inundated, 13-16
Chilean uplift, 19
Chimborazo, mount, 41
   possible eruption, 150-151
   ruins near, 35-36
Chinchasuyu road, 76
Chone river, 35
Chorlavi river, 55
Collasuyu road, 76
Colorado Tambo, Peru, identified with Judea, 140
Comnor, hill, 54
Continental divide, 16
Copper, discovered by Lehi's group, 64
Coquimbo, Chile, identified with Lehi's landing-place, 64

Cordillera Carabaya, 73
Cordillera Occidental, 35, 44, 46, 50, 55, 57
Cordillera Oriental, 35, 46, 57
Cordillera Vilcabamba, 73
Coriantumr, 36, 50-60
Corihor, rebellion and travels, 34-38
   valley of, 53
Coseguina, eruption of volcano, 150
Cowley, Matthew, story on Maori origins, 147
Cuenca, Ecuador, 30, 31
   in inter-Andean plain, 35
   on narrow neck, 27
Cumorah, hill, 53, 56-57, 155
Cumorah, land of, 43-44
Cumorah, north of narrow neck, 6
Cuntusuyu road, 76
Cuzco, Peru, 65, 70
   on Inca road, 68
   Inca road ran from, 27
   See also Hanan-Cuzco, Hurin-Cuzco

-D-

Darien Gap, lack of civilized remains in, 24
Darien, Isthmus of, 23-24
Darkness, three days of, 151
Darwin, Charles, 117
   confirms inundations in South America, 13-16
   describes volcanic eruption, 149-150
de la Vega, Garcilaso, Spanish chronicler, 65-67
The Incas, 71, 72, 83, 85
Desolation, city of, Lamanite attack on, 31
Desolation, land of, 24, 27, 29-32
   bordered on Bountiful, 30
   composition of, 32
   fortified at narrow pass, 154
   in relation to Bountiful, 1
   Moron near, 35
   part of narrow neck, 30
de Soto, Hernando, on Cuzco's Sun Temple, 71
Destruction, the great, narrow pass remained after, 29

-E-

Earthquakes, 150
East Island, 16-18
East Sea, 29, 33
   Amazon valley was, 10-12

back-filling of, 27
change of outlet, 19
East Sea South, 13-16
East Wilderness, 4-5, 126-129
Ecuador, place of Jaredite landing, 33
Encyclopaedia Britannica, on Amazon sea, 10-12
Eruptions, volcanic, and chain reactions, 149-150
Expedition, discovers Jaredite lands, 93

-F-

Flocks, Jaredite, flee to land southward, 47
Fortifications, in land of Bountiful, 147-148
of Nephite cities, 78

-G-

Geography, basic Book of Mormon, 1-6
Gid, city of, 134-135
Gideon, city of, 103-104
Gideon (Limhi's subject), leads Nephites from bondage, 93-96
Gideon, valley of, 103-104
Gilgal, valley of, 49-50
Gold, discovered by Lehi's group, 64
panned from Peruvian river, 78
Gordon, Cyrus H., *Before Columbus*, 16-18
on inscribed stone, 142-144
Gran Chaco Boreal, 16
Guaillabamba gorge, 44, 50, 54, 60
Guaillabamba river, 44
Guatemala, 146
Guayaquil, gulf of, 31, 32, 33, 40, 52
identified with narrow neck, 26-32
journey length to Loja, 27
Guayas, Ecuador, early pottery discovered near, 37
Guayas river, 31, 34, 35, 52
Guiana, highlands, 18
Gulf, at narrow neck, 26

-H-

Hagoth, ships built by, 3, 146-147
Hanan-Cuzco, 70, 84
identified with Shilom, 82-83
Hanson, Earl Parker, on ancient South American sea, 15
Hapgood, Charles H., *The Path of the Pole*, 117
Helam, land of, 91

Helam, people of, under Lamanite bondage, 96
Helaman, and stripling soldiers, 140
epistle to Moroni, 132
Hermoso, hill, could be hill Shim, 43
Hermounts wilderness, 106-107
Heshlon, plains of, 50
Heth, land of, 40-41
Hewett, Edgar L., *Ancient Andean Life*, 39, 100
Highland, inter-Andean, 34-35
History, rememberers of, 33, 43, 65
Huallaga river, 134
Huancayo, Peru, identified with Gideon, 103-104
Huanuco, Peru, identified with Nephihah, 132
Humboldt current, 80
Hurin-Cuzco, 71, 78, 82, 120
identified with city of Nephi, 70
temple and tower in, 84

-I-

Ica, Peru, 140
Imbabura, Ecuador, identified with waters of Ripliancum, 54-56
suggested land of Cumorah, 44-45
Imbabura, hill, identified with hill Cumorah, 56-57
Inca road, 67-70
avoided Montaro river, 101
ran through Loja, 27
Incas, 35, 38
Indians, white, in East Wilderness area, 129
Insects, plague of, in Nephi, 84-85
"Iron, Island of," 16-18
Ishmael, land of, 115-117
Isle of the sea, Nephites on, 9
Isthmus, narrow neck is, 29
at narrow neck, 26
Izcu-Chaca, Peru, identified with Minon, 104-106

-J-

Jacob, words on isles of the sea, 9
Jared, and companions, colonization by, 34
Jaredites, land of, 30
lands of, 33-48
things carried to America, 47
war zones of, 49-60

166 Index

Jauja-Huancayo valley, fortresses, 129
  identified with valley of Gideon, 103-104
Jauja, Peru, battle on suspension bridge, 106
  suspension bridge at, 103-104
Jershon, city of, 132
  land of, 121-124
Jerusalem, land of, 120
Jesus Christ, visitation of, 151-152
Jivaro, head hunters east of Andes, 46
Junin, lake, dimensions, 123
  headwaters of Montaro river, 101-103

-K-

Kotosh, Peru, identified with Lehi, 133-134

-L-

Lake country, of Ecuador, 44-45
Lamanites, converted, beautify Ishmael, 116
Land northward, 1, 23, 33
  Nephites driven into, 153-154
  possessed by Nephites, 30
  sometimes included Desolation, 30
Land southward, 1, 23, 30
  conquered by Lamanites, 154
  made ready for immigrants, 47, 64
  preserved by Jaredites for game, 31
Land, whole face of, changed, 149-151
Landing, Jaredite, 33-34
Landing, Nephite, 26
Lane, Frank W., *The Elements Rage*, 150
La Raya pass, 65, 73, 76, 77, 78, 120
Latacunga, Ecuador, 50, 52
Lehi, carried little food, 47
Lehi, city of, 133-134
Lehi, land south called, 4
Lehi, place of landing, 63-64
Lehi-Nephi, city of. *See* Nephi, city of
Lehi-Nephi, land of. *See* Nephi, land of
Lib, 52-53
Lightning, 150
Limhi, 83, 93
Loja, Ecuador, 29, 30, 31
  eastern point on narrow neck, 27
  entrance to Amazon, 26

-M-

Machala, Ecuador, near site of Jaredite city, 31
Machu Picchu, identified with Amulon, 88-90

Manabi, ancient race in Ecuador, 38
  identified with Jaredite culture, 39
Manaus, Brazil, depth of Amazon at, 12
Manco Capac, 73
  identified with Nephi, 65-67
Manta, Ecuador, 38, 41
Manti, land of, 109-111
Maoris, origins of, 147
Marañon river, 12, 135
Mayas, 38
Mayo river, 134
Mayoc, Peru, identified with Melek, 107
Means, Philip Ainsworth, *Ancient Civilizations of the Andes*, 33-34
Melek, land of, 107
Mendoza, Argentina, 14
  on Inca road, 68
Mendoza, Peru, possible location for Omner and Gid, 134-135
Mexicans, ancient, perhaps a remnant of Ammonites, 145-146
Mexico, 146
Middoni, land of, 119-120
Migrations, to land northward, 141-142
Minon, land of, 104-106
Mira river, 55
Mississippi river, waterway of colonization, 142
Montaro river, identified with Sidon river, 101
  Zarahemla's eastern boundary, 101
  U-turn housed Jershon, 123
Morianton, city of, 133-134
Mormon, 153-155
  Ammaron's words to, 43
Mormon, land of, 73, 90
Mormon, waters of, 90
Moron, city of, 37
Moron, land of, 38, 52, 60
  near Desolation, 35
  seat of Jaredite government, 34
  taken by Shared, 49-50
Moroni (chief captain), 126
  defense measures of, 4-5
Moroni, city of, 129-130, 132
Moroni (son of Mormon), last years of, 156-157
  records received from Mormon, 155
  use of geographical terms, 30, 43
Moronihah, 147
Mosiah I, 78-80
  discovery of Mulekites, 4
  interprets Coriantumr's stone, 60
Moyobamba, Peru, possible location of Gid, 134-135

Mulek, city of, 132
  retaken by stratagem, 135-137
Mulek, land north called, 4
Mulekites, discovered by Mosiah I, 4
  Coriantumr discovered by, 60

-N-

Narrow neck of land, 1, 23-32, 33, 35
  Jaredites built city by, 31
  term not used after Christ's visit, 29
  See also Paramos
Narrow pass, 24, 29
  Nephite-Lamanite boundary, 154
Narrow passage. *See* Narrow pass
Nazca, Peru, 76, 140
Nehor, city of, 45
  Jaredites ruled from, 38
Nephi, city of, 73, 78
  identified with Cuzco, 70
Nephi, clue to course of journey, 65-67
  identified with Inca legend, 65-67
Nephi, land of, 3, 73, 80-81
  in mountains, 3
  in relation to Zarahemla, 3-4
  nearly surrounded by water, 27
  part of land southward, 3
Nephihah, city of, 130-132
Nephite Island, 18, 19-20
  catastrophic changes throughout, 149-151
Nephites, closing wars of, 154-155
  trek from landing point, 10
Nile river, delta of, 19
Noah (Jaredite king), 40
Noah (Nephite king), 71, 83, 87
North America, colonization from South America, 142
  not an island, 10

-O-

Obidos, Brazil, breakthrough of Amazon at, 19
  depth of Amazon at, 12
Ogath, 56
Old Civilizations of the New World, A. Hyatt Verrill, 24, 38
Omer, 40
  journey of, 41
Omner, city of, 134-135
Onandagus, prophet, 144-145
Ore, refinement of, in Nephi's time, 77-78
  discovered by Lehi's group, 64

Orinoco river, 18
  delta of, 18-19
Oro, battle of, 29
Oro pass, 29, 54
  See also Narrow pass
Osorno, eruption of volcano, 150
Otavalo, Ecuador, 45
  identified with Ogath, 56

-P-

Pachacamac, Peru, 80
  identified with Zarahemla, 99
Pampas, 16
  of Argentina and Uruguay, 15
  seasonal flooding of, 15
Panama, 146
  not narrow neck area, 23-26
Paraguay, formerly inundated, 13-16
Paraiba river, inscribed stone found near, 16-18
Paramonga, Peru, near Hermounts, 106
  northern boundary of Zarahemla, 101
Paramos, 32
  of Ecuador, description, 30
Parana river, 15
Parsons, James J., on Amazon sea, 12
Pasto, Colombia, 76
  end of Inca road, 55-56
Patagonia, sea shells in, 13-14
Peru, coast of, 31
Pisac, Peru, 76
  identified with Antiparah, 140
Pisco, Peru, southern boundary of Zarahemla, 101
Pizarro, search for "Land of Cinnamon," 53
Plain, or plateau, between Cordilleras, 35
Plutarch, sailors' yarn recorded, 16
Portillo pass, Andes, 14
Pottery, pre-Inca, in Ecuador, 37
Pratt, Orson, statement on Lehi's landing-place, 64
Price, Willard, *The Amazing Amazon,* 13
Priests, of King Noah, 88-90
Puerto Bolivar, port of, 31
Puman-Chochan, Peru, identified with Ammonihah, 107-108

-Q-

Quipu-keepers, Inca, 33
Quito, Ecuador, 27, 44, 45, 52
  on Inca road, 68
  Pedro de Alvarado's route to, 41

Quito valley, identified with valley of Gilgal, 50
  in inter-Andean plain, 35
Qutimbo, towers at, 118

-R-

Rain forest, east Andean, 46
Ramah, hill. *See* Cumorah, hill
Ramah, meaning of, 56
Record-keepers, Inca, 33
Resort, Nephite word for fort, 83
Riobamba, Ecuador, 40, 41, 50, 52
Ripliancum, waters of, 54-56
  ruins near, 35
Riplah, hill, 126
Riplakish, fine goldsmith work done under, 39
Rocky mountains, 144-145
Ruins, Chile's no match for those in north, 64
Runners, Inca, 27

-S-

Sacsahuaman fortress, Cuzco, 83, 96
Sacsahuaman, hill, Cuzco, 76
Sailors, visit to South America, 60 B.C., 16-18
Salinas, Ecuador, Heth near, 41
Sampu. *See* Santa Elena
Samuel the Lamanite, 100
"San Luis Rey, bridge of," 76
Santa Elena, Ecuador, climatic conditions, 34
  landing-place of Indian forbears, 34
Santa Fe, sea once reached, 15
Santiago, Chile, 14, 64
  on Inca Road, 68
Saraguro, Ecuador, 29
Savoy, Gene, 149
Sea, ancient, in South America, 13-16
Sea East, 6
Sea North, 6
Sea South, 6
Sea West, 6
Seashells, beds of, in South America, 14-15
Sebus, waters of, 117
Serpents, poisonous, force Jaredite flocks southward, 30, 46-47
Shared, 49
  brother of, 52
Shemlon, land of, 73, 81, 87, 88, 91
Shilom, city of, 73
Shilom, land of, 81-82, 96

Shilom, meaning of Hebrew word, 83
Shim, hill of, 41, 43-44
  Ammaron buries records in, 43
  Mormon removes records from, 155
Shipping, 3
  basis of communication, 141-142
Shiz, 36, 53-60
Shule, 40
  ruled from Nehor, 38
Shurr, valley of, 54
Sidom, land of, 109
Sidon river, 5-6, 111
  head of, 5, 132
  on Zarahemla's eastern border, 101
Silver, discovered by Lehi's group, 64
Sister-wife, of Manco Capac, Inca legend, 65-67
Smith, Joseph, on Nephite lands, 10
  statement on Lehi's landing-place, 63-64
Sons of Mosiah, in land of Nephi, 115
South America, not an island, 10
  tilting of, 19
South Wilderness, 4
  of the Jaredites, 121
Stone, inscribed, found in Brazil, 16-18
Stone, skilled use of, in Cuzco, 72-73
Sun Temple, in Cuzco, 71
Sweet potatoes, native to South America, 147

-T-

Tabacundo, Ecuador, identified with valley of Corihor, 53-54
Taguando river, 55
Talca, Chile, 14, 76
  on Inca road, 68
Tambora, Indonesia, volcanic eruption, 150
Tarapoto, Peru, possible location of Omner, 134-135
Teancum, battle with Amalickiah, 135
Tehuantepec, isthmus of, not narrow neck area, 24-26
Temple, of Solomon, built of special stones, 71
Terrace-building, description, 108
Terraces, near Tiahuanaco, 117
Thrones, suggesting cultural similarities, 39
Thunder, 150
Tiahuanaco, identified with Ishmael, 117
Tierra del Fuego, Argentina, 14
Titicaca, lake, 65, 76, 77
  identified with waters of Sebus, 117
Tornadoes, 150

Totora reeds. *See* Balsas reeds
Tower, in city of Nephi, 81
Towers of the dead, around lake Titicaca, 118
Treasures, Incan, buried in cerro Hermoso, 43
Trees, petrified, near Mendoza, Argentina, 14-15
Trinidad, 18
Tulcán, Ecuador, 55
Tumbes, Peru, Hagoth's ships sailed from, 146
on Inca road, 68

-U-

Upano river, 27
Upheavals, at time of Christ, 18
"Up unto," significance of term, 34, 38
Urubamba river, 87
Uruguay, 18
formerly inundated, 13-16

-V-

Velikovsky, Immanuel, *Earth in Upheaval,* 116
Verrill, A. Hyatt, *Old Civilizations of the New World,* 24, 38
Verrill, A. Hyatt and Ruth, *America's Ancient Civilizations,* 38, 116, 145
Vilcabamba Cordilleras, 91
Vilcabamba, identified with Helam, 91
Vilcabamba the Old, lost Inca city, 88-90
Vilcabamba wilderness, 88, 91
denseness of, 96
Vicañota, lake, identified with waters of Mormon, 90-91
Vilcañota mountains, 73
Vilcañota valley, 65

Vilcas-Huaman, Peru, identified with Sidom, 109
von Hagen, Victor Wolfgang, *Ecuador and the Galapagos Islands,* 30
Highway of the Sun, 27, 70, 108, 118, 120
The Desert Kingdoms of Peru, 149

-W-

Wall, forty-mile, along Santa river, 147-149
Webb, Kempton E., on size of Amazon, 13
"Went over," significance of term, 38
Whirlwinds, 150
Williams, Frederick G., writing states Lehi's landing-place, 63-64
Wind furnaces, found in Peru, 77-78
Writing, style of, on Bat Creek stone, 142-144

-Y-

Yucatan, 146

-Z-

Zamora river, 26-27
Zarahemla, city of, burned but later rebuilt, 151
Zarahemla, land of, 3, 76, 99-111
fighting on west coast, 140
in relation to Nephi, 3
Mosiah I leads Nephites to, 78-80
nearly surrounded by water, 27
part of land southward, 3
Limhi's men bypass, 93
Zelph, the white Lamanite, 144-145
Zeniff, and group, in Nephi, 80
Zoramites with Lamanites, attack Nephites, 125-126